SOCIAL

BENCHMARKS

A Common Sense Critique of our Social and
Economic Systems.

Comments on this book are welcome to:
craigdhanks@aol.com

Contents

iv

INTRODUCTION

Just as surveyors have points of reference established on the land, called "Benchmarks" (a circle cut with an equal cross), from which all property lines, roads, utilities, and buildings can be located and planned. Likewise, in society there are principles of social interaction that are the Benchmarks that help us build and amend our social and economic structures, with bodies of law established to promote the freedom to adhere to those principles.

I am on a continuous search to discover and understand those social benchmarks, whose absence in our daily lives is replaced with the anger, hate, and selfishness that promote the decay and destruction of our societies. I say this because I perceive a definite lack of understanding of our social and economic structures; from your and my neighbors, as well as our political and educational leaders.

This book is presented to all who are as curious as I, to understand the social and economic principles that define our cultures and nations. It is my hope that the following pages will provide you with a better understanding of our current social-economic friction and its origins.

With the shrinking of our ignorance and isolation by research, new technology, much faster transportation of people, materials, and information, it is not too soon to re-examine those social relationships that give rise to wealth and poverty. Individuals, corporations, and nations are competing for dwindling resources in the face of greater consumption. This form of competition has most often led to wars in the past and continues in many parts of the world to bring about ethnic civil wars over ancient claims to land and resources.

I am not seeking to provide a blueprint for our social interactions of the future. Rather I hope to explain the present and past in a light that can make the planning of future social changes more certain of success. The ideas expressed in this book are not new. Many of them were popular and well trafficked in the schools of philosophy in previous centuries. They failed to take hold in our societies in the 1800's because social pressures to deal with economic oppression were diminished by the promise of industrialization, unlimited resources and unlimited wilderness for dissenters to occupy and control. Today, anti-social pressures are rising everywhere because technology is eliminating jobs that required skills and life-long commitment, reducing the economic security necessary for a stable social network for the working middle-class.

The arguments of this book are meant to be philosophical rather than technical. Most economists would exclaim upon reading this book that I am only stating the obvious. My readings of many books on economics, especially school texts, convince me that the whole realm of economics is put under scientific scrutiny to make it more and more technical, requiring great expertise to understand it. I seek to maintain the simple expression of historical economics, and to explain our modern creations of economic activities and investments in the simpler social, cultural and philosophical terms that are understandable to all. It is important to note that there are no purely economic issues; they are always intertwined with social and cultural issues. Differences of opinion on how societies should operate economically have led to a great deal of heated debate, as well as many wars. So I am certainly throwing caution to the wind in my effort to reduce our modern economic practices to simple social principles, some of which must be held accountable for their social defects. I thank you for your time spent reading this material and I hope you find it thoughtful and insightful.

Craig D. Hanks
Author

Chapter 1 - Defining the concept of money

Few people in our technically sophisticated western economies realize that what we call "mother nature" provides the great abundance of all that we consume in the form of minerals, plants and animals. The Earth has an annual growth cycle for plants and animals; and we harvest this produce to provide for our near future. How we share, or refuse to share, this natural produce and the Earth's mineral resources, has created the misery and poverty that surrounds us.

Human society did not and cannot start on a barren planet with only mineral resources. We require large surpluses of food and complex organic materials for clothes and shelters, provided to us for free, but for the labor of processing. And yet we divide and consume our portions in such discriminatory fashion, that wars, poverty and social unrest plague our planet. We suffer recessions, depressions, wars, economic domination, and periodic social chaos, because we have invented nations, exclusive societies, and exclusive economies; and empowered them with socio-economic alliances that feed off dominated nations and societies; enforcing discriminatory laws and alliances with police, courts, and military organizations.

As a rule we are almost all pre-occupied with the desire to amass wealth in the form we call money. We hope to receive more of the Earth's bounty even if others receive less. At the same time, we are striving as various politically independent societies for the social equality that eludes us for various reasons, many of which are tied to our belief that there is insufficient money available in our society to solve our social problems. We also believe, incorrectly, that our individual future security depends very much on the amount of money we will acquire, because we attach intrinsic value to money that does not exist.

The subject of money has always gotten a lot of attention. If we do not dwell on money personally, we certainly do discuss it with family and friends. We relate a person's social status to the quantity of money that he or she possesses. But money, as we are taught to understand and desire it, is an illusion, a socially destructive illusion.

There is no such thing as money or wealth, in the form of paper, plastic, or metal. These objects - dollars, checks, credit cards, gold and silver - that we call money are really only transfer agents for what money really represents; and as transfer agents they have no intrinsic value. So what is this money-wealth we want to amass and control? It is Labor, more specifically everyone's PRODUCTIVE LABOR. For human societies, Productive Labor is the only wealth in the universe! We consume the Earth and all that its environment provides; but only labor may harvest and transform the materials we consume. There is no other form of wealth; there is no other form of money than productive labor. The paper and plastic money we use is simply the exchange medium of productive labor. We know this when we exchange our labor for money (our paycheck), but we do not commonly realize that we can only exchange our labor-money for the goods and services of other people's labor. That is, we barter our productive labor to purchase the goods and services of other people's productive labor, by using money as the most widely accepted exchange medium.

To call money an illusion is to suggest that it does not exist, which flies in the face of reason, when anyone can pull a couple of dollars out of their pocket. The illusion is - our common perception that our paper dollars have value intrinsic to the paper itself, separate from productive labor. Every nation that distributes money, without regulating the quantity in circulation to reflect that nation's total production of goods and services, knows the fallacy of such a belief.

Most accountants and economists will say that the idea of money as an exchange for labor is about 200 years old, and that their college courses taught them this fundamental fact. However, they soon forget what money really is, and join the rest of society in worshipping money in place of productive labor, and thereby support this illusion of money-wealth in place of productive labor wealth.

All of our physical acts are a form of labor. At work, at play, at home, at the office, on the golf course, volunteering for a charity, doing time in jail, all such

4

acts are labor. Most of these labors are not suitable for exchange with others. Gossiping on the telephone or clicking through the channels of the TV are not to be compared with farming, manufacturing, teaching, etc. While many of our labors are directed toward fulfilling our personal wants and needs, these efforts are not rewarded with the labor receipt of money.

So the first great division in the concept of labor is that it is either socially productive or non-productive. Socially productive labor is that which can be exchanged for other productive labor or stored for future exchange and consumption. Even in the simplest society productive labor divides into two basic forms. First we have the labor necessary to sustain life; by choice or coercion we produce food, clothes and shelter. The second form of labor, also provided by choice or coercion, is surplus productive labor over and above the labor needed to sustain life. This form of labor is the chief reason we are able to develop and expand our civilization. Whatever labor we commit to producing goods over and above our immediate consumption, that will be traded with others for future goods and services, or kept for our own future consumption, is STORED productive labor. The control of productive labor and ownership of stored labor is the foundation of what we call wealth, and those who cannot acquire productive and stored labor to benefit themselves, help us to define poverty.

Our society has amassed a great deal of stored productive labor in the form of public buildings, schools, highways, railroads, bridges, dams, airports, homes, factories, office buildings, power plants, communication networks, etc. Much of this stored labor has been built up over several generations. Each succeeding generation has enjoyed the stored labor of its forbears, and built upon the stored labor that preceded it, creating the social resources we call our infrastructure. Besides our infrastructure we maintain significant, but shorter term, stored labor in our household appliances, and furniture, our automobiles, and many quality of life gadgets.

Our capacity to produce an abundance of goods, such that we are able to maintain significant surpluses of food, clothes, appliances, etc.; requires an instrument like gold or paper or plastic money that can remove ourselves and our employers from any need to barter our productive labor directly with other producers. By being paid a (universal) labor receipt, dollars, we may shop in the stores where much of our combined surplus is displayed and exchange our productive labor for other people's productive labor. This has led to our treating "Money" as a lubricant of economic activity, in place of productive labor.

Consider labor in a complex society like our own. Unlike simple hunter-gatherer societies, our cities and towns are conglomerations of many and varied types of labor. Many people cannot directly associate their labor with the transporting and transforming of the many resources that comprise our labor economy. While others labor directly with raw materials in industries where their labor is rewarded for time spent at the job, not for the amount of goods produced. These limitations cause us to view our wages as something separate from the productivity of our labor. This also skews our value system for labor in general; it causes us to desire the reward of greater consumption for less production, without realizing that in the totality of our economy, more for one means less for another. It also causes us to grow up with an unnatural desire to receive the benefit of others labor, defining a successful person as one who receives very much in the form of labor receipts (dollars), for doing very little in the form of productive labor.

Money, in various forms, has been around since before recorded history. It performs three basic services for societies, each of which is only one form or another of Productive Labor. The first and most common use of money is as a medium for exchange, allowing us to work and exchange our labor for dollars that we then exchange for the labor-goods and labor-services that maintain our lives. Second, the long-term ability of dollars to act as an exchange medium is based on the dollar's ability to serve as a unit of account. We set reasonably stable dollar costs for our labor and for the goods and services we wish to purchase. All of our productive labor, starting with raw materials from the Earth, to processing in various ways, to advertising and distributing for consumption, is related within our economy by stipulating the value of each phase of productive labor in dollar amounts. This allows us to spend our paycheck in any manner we choose and still get a relatively equivalent return of goods and services from others labor, because we all accept and use the dollar to define the exchange value of our labor. The third service that money provides for us is that it is a store of value. If we do not need to spend our wages for immediate consumption and choose instead to hold those dollars for some time into the future, they will still purchase goods and services from the overall surplus, without loss of value. Except for the effect of inflation or deflation, money maintains its exchange value for future productive labor and thereby becomes our primary store of value. This store of value is also why we worship the dollar rather than productive labor. We define our productive labor in terms of dollars, rather than define dollars in terms of productive labor. If dollars were always viewed in terms of the labor they represent, then when we encountered people who had millions of dollars, we could properly ask, from whom did they acquire that surplus productive labor?

The third function of money, as a "store of value", is actually the source of the illusion of money representing wealth. Because of its – apparent but miss-understood - ability to hold purchasing power into the future, money is desired by everyone in place of continuous labor. If the amount of goods and services that will be produced in the future is stable, and if the amount of dollars available to facilitate the exchange of future goods and services is also stable, then our money can represent a store of value that can be exchanged in the future, for future goods and services. However, if the supply of dollars is changing; if the supply of goods and services is changing; if the demand for goods and services is changing; then the value of money is also changing. The value that can be stored in money has to do with our ability to continue to produce goods and services; and not in any esoteric wish or belief associated only with the paper or plastic money itself.

Historically, the most familiar money in the Western World was gold and silver, which came back into use in Europe and the Mediterranean area around the twelfth century, following the so-called Dark Ages. Although Roman Empire had coin-money to allow for more efficient internal trade and labor exchange, the Dark Ages reduced labor exchange to mainly local bartering, with very little exchange between diverse and distant cultures. The European Renaissance brought about expanded production (stored surplus labor) and expanded trade, which promoted invention and greater efficiencies that continue to this day. Today we have replaced gold and silver with paper dollars and checks, as well as advancing credit to consumers through credit cards and bank loans; allowing such debts to be repaid by printed dollars or checks that we receive as wages, or profits, or charity.

Without a universal medium of exchange, a cabinetmaker for example, wanting to sell his services to a corn farmer could not do business unless he was willing to take corn in trade. Unable to strike a deal, they could go to a barter style marketplace and attempt to find enough people with other surplus goods and sufficient needs to allow the farmer to exchange corn with others who had things the cabinet maker valued, in trade for which he would build cabinets for the farmer. In this manner, the farmer could barter his labor for the labor of the cabinetmaker. The pace and productivity of our contemporary labors would be greatly hampered if we had to exchange our productive labor in a similar manner.

Problems like this were overcome hundreds of years ago by designating certain commodities (gold and silver, for example), which were in limited supply and difficult to counterfeit, to be the medium of exchange. The marketplace would establish values relative to gold and silver for all commodities and services. In essence, and in fact, the amount of gold and silver that were exchanged in an economy yearly was equal to the amount of labor (goods and services) brought to the marketplace yearly. The amount of gold and silver in circulation in such a society always equals the productive labor made available for sale by its citizens. If the amount of labor made available to a marketplace increased while the amount of gold or silver was static or declining, everyone would receive less gold and silver for their labor. But they would likewise be paying less for the labor of others, because labor barters for labor and gold and silver were simply a means of labor exchange. If the amount of gold and silver coming to the marketplace were to increase, people would ask more for the products of their labor, and consequently they would pay more for the products of other people's labor. Although prices would change with increases or decreases in exchange money, such a cash marketplace would be static in the value of labor being exchanged, and not really inflationary or deflationary.

Since the total consumption in a society is limited to the total productive labor-goods and labor-services available to be consumed, the amount of exchange money available to facilitate trading can only partially inhibit or promote consumption in a cash economy. Exchange will occur in one manner or another using different kinds of money, or even direct exchange of goods without money. Even today, when people can barter directly, trading goods or services with others for different goods or services, they will do so without the use of paper or plastic money.

Although all nations have developed money-currencies to facilitate trade for consumption amongst their citizens, trade between nations requires that goods and services be bartered for goods and services. A reasonable balance of trade must be maintained, or nations will cease trading with those who produce nothing of barter value to the world economy.

To understand the relationship of productive labor and our paychecks, consider what would happen if all the farmers and manufacturers stopped working and went on government welfare, receiving a monthly welfare check to support them. For the first couple of weeks we would not notice much more than that the stores were sold out on some goods. By the second month there would be very little to buy. But since most of us would have government paychecks, we would be inclined to offer more and more of this free money for the dwindling supply of goods. As the government kept increasing the money needed to supply our paychecks, our dollar's exchange value would drop rapidly because there would be so few goods available and so many dollars competing to consume those goods. Since no one would be doing productive labor our currency would decline to worthlessness; it would lose its ability to be a store of labor-value. Since we would no longer be laboring to produce goods and services to exchange with others, we would not need any form of exchange money. To consume we must produce, both today and in the future. Any medium that we choose to be called money can only be an exchange medium, allowing us to more widely exchange the fruits of our labor for the fruits of others labor. Money can only facilitate the exchange of goods and services; it cannot maintain or represent a value other than productive labor.

What if, instead of some of our citizens having to remain unemployed, we put them to work making widgets? Since they now have jobs we can assume that society will flourish because of full employment. But Widgets, by definition, are useless contraptions, and since they are useless, no one, not even widget-makers, will barter their labor to consume them. Therefore, these workers would be unable to barter their widget-making labor. It would have to be considered unproductive labor; no different than the welfare they were on before they became widget makers. Labor must be productive, it must accomplish or assist in the production of some social material goal. Simply having a job does not necessarily benefit the rest of society. On the contrary, as make-work projects and bureaucracies grow, they inhibit the success of our collective endeavors. Those who labor at unproductive jobs, like welfare recipients, must receive their sustenance from the contributions of others that do labor productively.

To define the notion of money as labor in a more fundamental way, consider the Earth and its resources. Minerals, gas and oil, water, trees, farm and pastureland, wild and domestic animals, etc., all were here long before us. Although we put dollar values on these resources, they are really without value. The value we attach to them comes from the many uses we have discovered for these resources. These uses have all entailed lesser and greater amounts of our labor to transform and control them, and lesser and greater amounts of our labor being bartered for the opportunity to consume the Earth's resources.

Consider the building of a home out of refined wood products. Outside of its intrinsic value in the eco-

10

system a tree in the forest has no value in any human society, because we have not invested any labor to create the tree, or to transform the tree into food, clothes, shelter, transportation or communication. To use a tree, we must first create a log. We do this by cutting down the tree and removing the limbs. Creating the log has required that we destroy the tree. Therefore, the value of the log is equal to the labor it took to transform it from its natural state as a tree. We now have to transport the log to a place where it can be refined into wood products. Our road building labor and our transport labor add additional labor value to the log - a log at the mill is worth more exchange-labor than a log in the forest. After we transport the log to a lumber mill, we destroy the log to create lumber and other products, adding more labor value. When the uniform boards and timbers are transported from the mill to a building site and transformed into a home, the uniformity and availability of the lumber are destroyed. In transforming the free resource of a tree into a house, or many and varied other products, we have labored with the tree and the other resources on the planet. The total labor that has gone into manufacturing and transporting the parts as well as the whole is the cost that must be paid for with the buyer's labor. Profit and interest on borrowed labor are the other costs. When we get a loan to build a house, we are not paying for trees or oil or mineral ores (etc.), we are borrowing the labor of the loggers, transporters, mill workers, builders and the manufacturers of all of the parts and appliances that make up a house. All of these laborers are being supported by the surplus goods and services available in our society at that time, and we are in debt until we can return to society an equivalent amount of our labor in the form of surplus goods and services that we specialize in providing.

In our day-to-day economy, the continuing demand for lumber by consumers (i.e. their willingness to barter goods and services in order to consume lumber) causes the lumberyard to order lumber from the mill, which causes the mill to purchase logs from logging companies, which causes loggers to seek more trees to harvest. Substitute any other resource for this tree example and the same economic relationship

11

applies.

This reasoning may seem to over simplify what appears to be a sophisticated and complex system of people and equipment at work. But it is important to realize that all of our machines, energy, tools and structures are products of labor, and only labor, applied to the free natural resources used to create them. Both in total, and in each minute part, all machines and structures, regardless of how complicated they may appear, and regardless of how many other machines and industries were required to create them, are only the result of our labor transforming the natural resources of the planet. There are only two ingredients in everything that we consume - material from the Earth and our productive labor. Our hands and minds are the means of transformation. Our food comes from our environment through the labor of farmers. Our clothes come from fibers made from animal, vegetable or mineral resources. The metals and minerals from which we construct buildings, machines, roads and bridges are taken from the environment. These materials were provided to us free. We need only invest the labor of transforming them to our needs.

A conglomeration of industries, built up over the years, gives the illusion that those industries, and their products, are only partially our labor, and partially something we do not generally understand. That unknown something is really only a different form of labor, labor from the past, which has been stored in roads, utilities, buildings, machines, tools, and technical knowledge. Stored labor gives us the opportunity to expand our industrial abilities by building on the past. If we use tools or factories that were provided by the labor of our ancestors, then we are increasing our standard of living by not having to invest our labor to produce those tools and factories. Our standard of living today depends very much on the labor of our ancestors, as well as our own labor to maintain and expand it. No payment of what we call money has ever been made to the Creator for rent, purchase, use or abuse of the Earth's resources. We consume the Earth without consulting a catalog, placing orders for goods, receiving invoices, and making money payments. The Earth is given to us, as is. It is only our labor, along with the

Creator's labor, which transforms resources into useful products. Paper and plastic money are just necessary tools to help us exchange the various fruits of our labor. The resources were meant to be free and available to those who have responsible needs. Labor was meant to be exchanged with labor for goods and services, or to be donated to those unable to offer any labor for the goods and services they require.

Assuming that our United States economy is a 10-Trillion Dollar economy (Gross Domestic Product) in 2006; and that 130-Million people are employed full time to produce that 10-Trillion Dollars, then the average value of a year's labor is about $77,000.00 per worker, in 2006. If in a moral sense each worker's labor is equal in fair value to the labor of every other worker, then we may calculate the percentage that we are paid annually relative to the average wage of $77,000.00 per year. Obviously we do not all receive this wage. Our economy operates on the principle that many must receive less so that some may receive more. In our present economy some are able to siphon off great amounts of our collective productive labor, which they can exchange for other products of our labor, or hold for future consumption. If one person labors full time at the Federal Minimum Wage and receives $11,500 annually to exchange for food, clothes, shelter, and recreation, while another labors likewise and receives $115,000, and yet a third person labors likewise and receives $1,150,000; we must conclude that we use structural inequality in our social economy to control opportunities to labor and to consume the products of our labor. All three of these workers can be equally productive, but in our pyramid economy many have a large portion of their productive labor taken to benefit the relative few who control our economy and resources; because a relative few in every business control who will work, as well as determine what amount of each worker's productive labor they will be allowed to keep.

In a similar manner amongst nations, the levels of productivity differ so much that some nations are very affluent, while others are extremely poor. Many factors influence the wealth of nations, not the least of which are economic alliances that are somewhat exclusive, and not above discriminating against countries not in their alliance. Both resources and technology are selfishly hoarded.

The German and Japanese economies of the 60's, 70's, and 80's are good examples of prosperity through great labor. Both Germany and Japan were industrial powers prior to World War II, but they lacked raw material resources to fuel their economies, and were being manipulated economically by other Colonial powers, which supplied or denied resources. After W.W.II (with outside help, mostly from U.S. capital and commodities), these countries had the access they had always desired to raw material resources. Old barriers were broken by the pressure of war debts, allowing the sale of commodities, upon which they were able to unleash their industrial know-how. For Germany and Japan, internal consumption supported by the exporting of surplus labor in exchange for additional raw material to expand internal production and consumption has contributed greatly to these nations high standard of living, at the expense of those nations that provide raw resources to them.

In contrast, we see in the oil producing countries the economic power available from controlling resources. In the case of OPEC, we saw the Middle Eastern countries exporting oil and some refined products rather cheaply, until the world's demand, and politics, caused this commodity to achieve a high value in terms of surplus labor. The energy available to power machines and increase labor productivity was controlled by certain countries, allowing those countries to exchange their crude oil for a share of the productive labor of our machines, which consume their oil. Since our machines could produce many times more goods than our hand labor, we are willing to trade part of their productivity for the energy that keeps them running.

The great increase in surplus labor that flowed to the Middle East in exchange for oil was bartered for the many products of our labors: improved domestic services and infrastructure, vast acquisition of armaments, purchases of resources overseas, investment in property and corporations overseas. Most importantly however, many OPEC countries invested in the refinement and transportation of the raw resource, oil, thereby controlling this commodity from ground to final consumer, benefiting from the labor exchanged along this whole chain. The commodity is free to those who live on top of it, but the labor which can be gathered and controlled by its demand is not only immense, it is the proof of where material wealth is derived (labor) and how it maintains itself (control of resources and their consumption to acquire surplus labor).

Every nation has its own domestic currency, and trade amongst nations is accomplished by calculating exchange rates between their internal currencies. Exchange rates are calculated by comparing the amount of domestic currency that is paid for equal amounts of productivity. Exchange rates are also affected by the amount of natural resources brought to world markets when importing countries must buy the exporting country's domestic currency to pay for such resources. The control of values associated with any currency is the relationship of productive labor and resources coming to market and the amount of domestic currency provided by government treasuries to facilitate the bartering of labor and resources.

However, there are numerous other instruments of labor value, which are difficult for governments and central banks to control. Today much of our money takes the form of corporate and personal promissory notes, which we call checks, credit cards, letters of credit and corporate bonds. In the past a nation's economy would be temporarily stifled if the supply of gold did not increase with growing populations and increased production Likewise, that economy could be temporarily inflated if too much new gold came into its markets to purchase limited goods and services. But in today's world, where most money (labor) transactions are made using checks and credit cards, the government can only control the amount of money in circulation through the private banking system. When individuals, businesses, and even government agencies pay their labor-debts with checks and credit cards, and receive their labor-income in the form of checks and credit card payments, then the quantity of money in circulation can be expanded even against the wishes of government. To control money supply requires that we control credit; and this is done through interest rates on that credit.

To exercise some form of control on money supply, the Federal Reserve System, attempts to control money supply, and unfortunately productive labor, by controlling bank interest rates on our savings and our loans. The Federal Reserve System is a private bank owned by some of our private commercial banks. The United States has no government owned banks; all banks are privately owned. The Federal Reserve exercises control over banking by numerous operating regulations and by controlling the amount of cash banks have available to do business. The Federal Reserve sells government bonds, at profitable interest rates, to the banks to remove cash (credit) from the economy and it buys them back to add cash (credit), as the need arises. The amount of credit dollars added or removed from the system inversely affects the interest rates charged for those credit dollars; influencing the actions of borrowers. Interest rates on loans are the main control available to Government to control labor-money supply.

One travesty of our self-government is that we have a Federal Reserve that can only attempt to control banking activities via interest rates on a nation-wide basis. Because our banks are private profit-making businesses, rather than a government service like the Department of Agriculture, or Commerce, or the Food and Drug Administration, or National Transportation. If banking were a government corporation, the Federal Reserve could control the money supply and economic activity by taking capital (surplus labor-dollars) from areas that are abusing it and investing that capital in areas that need it, i.e. interest rates would be intentionally higher or lower in certain areas of the country that required help in slowing or expanding growth; without disparaging other parts of our country by using those interest rates as a brake or gas-peddle on the whole economy.

When the economy is sluggish and under-productive the Federal Reserve can coerce the commercial banking system to increase credit and lower the cost of that credit by lowering interest rates that banks pay to borrow from the Federal Reserve banks, or by buying back government bonds from Federal Reserve

16

banks, providing them with more dollars to lend. That is, when banks have surplus cash that will not receive a profitable rate of interest from the Federal Reserve they will lower their lending rates. This encourages businesses to refinance loans for lower costs or borrow additional capital at lower costs to expand production, hiring more workers, whose labor and paychecks expand both production and consumption. Maximum employment is as important to increasing consumption as it is to increasing production and reducing government handouts to idle citizens. If the economy remains sluggish the Federal Reserve can simply create cash (credit) and infuse it into the economy through commercial banks to promote more borrowing and business expansion (to promote both additional production and consumption).

When the economy is booming from the effects of too much credit, inflation can result when prices rise to consume the dollars that are available. The Federal Reserve seeks to control such inflation by regulating bank interest rates to reduce the amount of credit available in the banking system for businesses, laborers and consumers to trade amongst themselves. This slows the expansion of consumption, and shortly thereafter the expansion of production. The Federal Reserve can pull out surplus cash by raising reserve requirements for commercial banks and by selling them bonds that give a good profit with no risk. If this is done timely and sufficient for the current economic conditions, the economy will expand and regulate itself by supply and demand. All that the Federal Reserve is trying to accomplish is to keep the dollars available to be exchanged equal to the amount of labor available to be exchanged. If our economy runs out of new labor to hire for additional production, then it must make do or suffer the effects of individual companies using their own capital to offer higher wages to hold their labor force until they can raise prices to compensate for such moves. Such action by the Federal Reserve to control money supply necessarily includes all dollars: currency, checks, credit cards, and numerous forms of financing new debt.

Although we desire equilibrium between production and consumption to affect stability and hopefully prevent poverty, such a situation seldom occurs for more than a very short period. Nature itself can vary greatly in both food production and weather or geological extremes. Our own labors and consumption can be greatly affected by the doings of the environment. In agriculture, over-production via bumper crops are offset at times by droughts, floods, freezing and insects, causing major crop failures; the farmer is hurt both by bumper crops depressing prices and crop failure eliminating a crop to sell. In our economy the farmer is forced to operate as an independent business, subject not only to the uncontrollable variables of production, but also forced to compete for consumption demand with other producers in a market whose consumption demand is quite inflexible. Our food is not only to a great degree perishable, but we do not expand consumption when supply is increased; we only change our buying patterns to take advantage of value. And because of these factors, farmers live in constant economic peril.

Labor surpluses and labor shortages also disrupt manufacturing and consumption. Wars and political unrest strain our economic output and redirect our production away from individual consumption. The dynamics of our economy require that we constantly adjust our productivity and how it is distributed. A static population requires, in the very least, static productivity, whereas a growing population must increase overall productivity to match increasing overall consumption demands. From a production-consumption standpoint, if all laborers double their production in a given period then they will be able to double their consumption also. If overall labor productivity increases, but consumption by labor is static or declining (reflected in a reduced standard of living for laborers), then that increased productivity has been diverted to be consumed by others that do not labor, or exported to gain higher profits from foreign consumers.

We the people can also create new money for the economy, by issuing and exchanging additional credit in our economy. The manner in which check writers and credit card users can increase the money supply is founded on the economic principle of profit, or more correctly, surplus productive labor. New money is created when manufacturers and retailers issue new credit to consumers who have no current money (labor) to offer in payment for surplus goods. The seller takes the buyer's promissory note (credit card, loan contract) and uses it as money, operating as a bank would. By selling these promissory notes into the labor-money exchange system, more exchange money circulates than should exist. When prices fail to fall on goods and services that are in over supply, which in a strictly cash economy they must, the artificial demand caused by creating additional credit, creates that additional exchange money.

When credit is extended to a laborer who then promises future labor money to consume a surplus today; that promise is treated as ready cash and is absorbed by the economy as a whole as soon as that credit is given. This increases the money supply and will result in inflation if a balancing deflation is not created elsewhere in the economy. Overproduction by industries that can afford to extend credit becomes a boon for them and a bust for other parts of our economy.

Debts arise from borrowing against past surpluses. The return to the economy of any production over and above the current supply of money to continue our economic transactions will be new surplus labor, i.e., new money. It will cause inflation of prices in whatever areas of the economy that it is exchanged. If it is spent overseas it will cause price inflation overseas. If it is mainly directed toward purchasing real estate it will inflate the price of real estate. If it is directed toward ownership of commodities and resources it will inflate the costs of commodities, resources and the products made from them. If it is directed to owning stocks and bonds and other speculative items, it will inflate the cost of those items at no benefit to our productive economy.

The collective money derived from recent profits, over and above costs, losses and previous profits for the whole economy, is new loan money or new credit money. This new money causes headaches for those who wish to control inflation. The removal of this new money from the economy by the Federal Reserve could be very hard on marginally profitable businesses, which must borrow to maintain production and which cannot survive increased interest rates brought on by Federal Reserve intervention. When some businesses or individuals over-produce and increase credit, other businesses or individuals must suffer increased losses equivalent to the new credit or new money is created within the economy, disturbing the overall equilibrium and causing inflation. When the government decides to not tax businesses and individuals on their increased productivity (new money), but then decides to let banks increase the cost of borrowing money for everyone, to absorb and control that new money, it does so at the expense of businesses and individuals who are not producing increased goods (new money). It amounts to favoritism by the bankers, supporting strength at the expense of weakness. Because Federal Reserve action through interest rates will cause losses, in weak industries and individual companies, equivalent to new profits throughout the economy generated by strong industries. Businesses that are not at fault for the creation of this new money; are the sacrifice by those in control of the economy, to allow those who create this new money to multiply its value. The stronger corporations become lenders to the weaker companies, or purchasers and liquidators of their weaker competitors.

New check money and new credit-card money are not counterfeit money, though the way we attempt to control new money disparages some parts of the economy as though it were counterfeit. To understand what is happening in different sectors of the economy we need to sort through the camouflage that the dollar puts on our economic activity. Rather than look at the dollar as universal money we need to see our economy as made up of ongoing labor-productivity money, and stored surplus labor in the form of debt money, investment money, speculation money, overseas US dollar money, tax welfare money and tax infrastructure money. With all of this money coming from our myriad sources of productivity and being spent to consume different goods and services, the attempt by the Federal Reserve to limit the growth or shrinkage of one type of money in our economy, puts blanket controls on all types of money in our economy.

One very socially damaging effect of our manner

of controlling new money is that we somehow disdain full employment. Rather than reduce the labor necessary to provide a decent living for everyone, while having an abundance of goods for all to consume, we choose to reduce the amount of labor in the overall economy by having some continue to labor forty hours per week and others to not labor at all. Using the level of unemployment as a gauge of current economic activity. It is fundamental to our form of capitalism, that in order for us to have a stable economy for the middle class, some citizens must have less and live in privation so that others can have more and live in affluence. It approaches slavery to require people to labor a certain number of hours per day over and above the amount actually given to them as wages. While those hours of productivity are taken and used by those who are forced to be non-productive, but must still be provided with material comforts.

Today we view the reduction of jobs in our society as a catastrophe. We worry about defense industry cutbacks because of the jobs that will be lost. We worry about changing technology because of the impact on people whose current skills will be replaced by machines. We worry about having state and federal prisons forming manufacturing facilities to rehabilitate prisoners into productive citizens, because we know other people will lose jobs in competing industries. We are so backward in our manner of controlling labor and sharing labor, that job loss is the number-two terror in our lives, right behind being a victim of crime. The further down the economic ladder, the more desperate we are to keep a job, while those at the top seek more and more leisure, to spend the labor wealth that comes to them from the productive labor of others. While we desire in our hearts to be secure from want and to enjoy endless leisure, we live in fear and dread of being unemployed. We live this schizophrenia because we are ignorant and selfish at all levels of society and all levels of international interaction regarding resources, trade, and manufacturing jobs.

One of the fundamental principles of technological economics is called the "division of Labor". This is the social structure wherein laborers are trained to be proficient in one skill only, becoming highly productive in their skill; but also very dependent on other laborers to produce all of the goods that they are unable to produce for themselves. In cultures that are viewed as primitive, the division of labor is usually limited to the gender boundary. Where young men learn all the ways of the hunt and of community defense, such that each male becomes competent to perform all such tasks in the male domain. Likewise for women, each young woman must learn to accomplish all tasks considered to be in the female domain. This does not mean that the better hunters, or arrowhead makers, or basket weavers will only provide for themselves, or will profit at the community's expense by bartering their talents for the products of others. Certainly talents are recognized and lend themselves to a slight division of labor, but in tribal communities such divisions are not structural. When the talented individual ages or dies, the community loses their contribution, which must be made up by the labor of others. The lack of a labor structure in such communities and the tradition of offspring marrying into other families, producing a community gene pool, allow special talents to come forth from any member of the community. There will be no hereditary powers concentrated in one family. No hierarchy of labors, divided to produce a surplus, controlled and consumed by hereditary leaders.

In what are called advanced societies the division of labor principle is credited as being the key to their advancement. Over the past thousand years it has become common for the European societies to develop and export this system through colonial domination. Though some may think that increasing populations cause the development of societies engaging in division of labor, such is not the case. Certainly a large population is required in order to develop and maintain a system engaging in division of labor, but a large population does not require division of labor, it only permits it to be developed as one form of social structure. When division of labor does occur, a society will experience a change in its density of population, such that large cities will develop to support the efficiencies of labor division.

If population increases beyond the capacity of its local environment to supply resources for that society, one of two things must happen; either that community must split into two groups requiring that one or both groups immigrate to new areas where they may maintain themselves without creating the social structure of division of labor; or if such a community grows in population and remains in the same location, then greater efforts must be expended in hunting and transporting resources over greater distances, as well as the development of agricultural industries as opposed to simple gathering of fruits and grains of smaller societies. Such pressures to develop complex supply systems require that individual labor becomes group labor and that group labor becomes specialized, to provide goods and services without waste or in a random manner. And thus division of labor is both permitted and required to maintain dense population groups.

Our large cities and nations are the culmination of this system. As we advance in manufacturing and transportation technology, we allow ourselves to maintain larger and larger populations in relatively small land areas (socially unhealthy densities). Division of labor promotes division of consumption, which causes division of freedom, opportunity and security, which promotes social unrest, crime, moral decay, and ultimately social destruction.

A society that chooses to grow in population, using division of labor, must have leadership and a government that is sufficient to the needs of its citizens. A simple system of one chief with a few advisors making all decisions regarding provisions for their tribe, as well as engaging in the daily labors themselves, will not work for larger groups. As a group gains population above a few thousand, they have become too large to see themselves as one extended family. They will remain strangers to many others in their group. And they will seek guidance and leadership from those chosen to lead, whose labor will be to make laws, keep records and direct the labors of its citizens to produce goods and services.

Once labor is divided and specialized and controlled to produce large quantities of foods and other goods, the division and distribution of food and other goods will not necessarily proceed according to need. History records the coming and going of hundreds of societies. In essentially all cases the leaders of all societies view themselves as elite, above the law, and the maker of law. These governments not only control the labors of their citizens, they tax those labors to provide goods and services for themselves, their armies, and the bureaucracies that facilitate their control over their population. Along with the development of the principle of division of labor has come the notion of wealth founded in the perversion of government when individual wealth controls the "division of consumption".

In less developed societies and many advanced societies the division of labor is broken into two major groups, menial or specialized. Menial labor is essentially slave labor, citizens without talents or education are required to accomplish all tasks that require exhaustive physical labor, and they are paid minimum wages that will barely sustain them. Those who perform specialized labors are made the taskmasters of the menial laborers; they become managers and builders of their society's infrastructure. Their wages and level of consumption provide them with some surplus to live a more secure life. This surplus comes from the abundance of food and fiber provided by nature and the menial labor used to gather and process it. At this level of division of consumption both groups labor daily, but one group receives much more for their time at labor than the other, and they receive that extra at the expense of the lower group. Some must have less so that others may have more.

Another great pitfall in the disparity of consumption arising from the division of labor is that in modern societies, changes in technology make the specialized labor of many workers obsolete. They loose their jobs and many fall into poverty while the developers and owners of the technology that displaced those workers gain wealth and profits to live in ease and luxury without regard to any consequences. The safety net of unemployment insurance, seldom lasting longer than six months, is paid at or below a subsistence level, and is raised by taxing the labor of employed workers. Those who are unable to labor because of age, disability, or lack of skill are maintained at a minimum subsistence level by a welfare system. Essentially, the society of those who labor productively is taxed for a portion of its products to support a welfare system to avoid moral guilt and social chaos. Such taxes cannot eliminate the prospect of social chaos. They can only postpone it until the vagaries of our environment swell the numbers on welfare to a point where our productive labor cannot support them and brings about revolution and change.

As far as the elite leadership, they receive and consume goods and services provided by all laborers. They take what they want, with little regard for the privation of the lower classes. They maintain their authority by perversion of the law and suppression of dissent by police organizations that perform as they are ordered without questioning those orders. It only takes a small police force to control a large population.

Societies are coerced or persuaded to depend on leadership by a few. Most choose to be followers and they choose to follow the established leadership unless it threatens to undertake their destruction. Even when civil unrest is widespread, those who seek change are promoting a few new leaders who promise change. The establishment need only control such renegade leadership to quell the unrest, so that misery and injustice may continue to be the norm.

The perversion of the division of consumption is entrenched in all populous societies. The United States was born with this principle in place, a million slaves and a hundred thousand indentured servants in a total population under five million, belies the breadth and scope of this new government, then hailed by freeborn merchants and frontiersmen.

Even today we do by law and economic institution maintain a division of consumption that is in no way related to the labors contributed to provide goods and services for consumption. But there is no other way for dense populations to operate. A fair distribution of goods and services requires that laborers live in small autonomous groups (tribes or congregations), where all citizens labor to produce what they consume and to share freely with others.

MONEY? Goods and services cannot be had for money. They can only be had in trade for other goods and services; earned, borrowed, begged, or stolen.

Chapter 2 - Economic predation and social problems of money

The abundance of life and life-giving sustenance on our planet is supported by a principle of interaction that sets the tone and demeanor for all life forms to interact. That principle is PREDATION. Every life form is a predator and preys on other life forms. By occupying territory and crowding out others, by killing competitors if necessary, by consuming other life forms to sustain themselves, and by being subject to being killed and consumed by other predators. Predation exists all up and down the life-chain, beginning with the very simplest one-cell plants and viruses. Surpluses of life forms are mandatory in this system and balance is maintained, not with steady state precision, but by any increases or decreases in one life-form contributing to increases or decreases in the life forms that prey on and depend on the first life-form.

There are two apparent hierarchies of available food. First is the plant system, the very smallest of plants in the ocean form the foundation of the entire ocean predation system. While on land, the smallest of plants and quasi-plant-animal organisms facilitate the conversion of minerals into compounds which larger and more complex plants need to survive and reproduce their generations of life. Certainly there is some symbiosis within the plant system, the animal system, and crossovers between plants and animals; this however, does not belie the principle of predation, on the contrary it shows how allies can be more effective predators as well as protectors of their particular specie and habitat.

The other hierarchy of predation is the animal system, wherein many species of animals are strictly plant eaters and do by size and numbers consume a great deal of the plant life available. Another part of the animal system consumes only other animals, the so-called carnivores. Typically carnivores do not eat other carnivores; rather they eat the plant eaters; and there are a few animals that consume both plants and animals

as they come upon them. Though there are some
primitive life forms that reproduce "life" from heat and
or light and minerals, everything else, including most
bacteria and viruses, are consuming other life forms in
order to create and sustain themselves. Life begets life,
life transforms life, and life consumes life, through
predation only.

What about mankind? So far we are the ultimate
predators on Earth. We dominate and manipulate the
animal, vegetable, and mineral systems. We have
developed the ability to destroy much of the animal and
vegetable systems on Earth, and we have certainly
upset the balance of predation that has controlled life
on Earth before our developing technologies. We have
upset the balance of predation for most of the higher
animals and plants. We have polluted the upper and
lower atmosphere, the oceans, most lakes and rivers, as
well as depleted or polluted many aquifers of ground
water. Our activities have led to the disappearance of
many species of plants and animals, and it is not certain
that our actions will be within our control over the long
run.

Some questions we need to answer; are we
constrained within the balancing mechanism of nature?
Or does our ability to alter genetics as well as leave the
Earth and move into space, place us beyond the natural
balancing mechanisms? Is mankind capable of sharing
the Earth with other life forms? And are we working
towards equal standards of consumption for everyone,
distinguished only by the practicalities of location and
natural resources? How radical will our social predation
of productive labor go before we experience outright
chattel slavery, civil wars, and revolutions?

Surplus labor in the form of stored labor is the
primary reason for the expansion of civilization, both in
population and knowledge. History indicates that our
social expansion has come at a great price. The
calamities associated with the predatory control of
surplus labor, throughout history, have caused the
majority of all people, at all times, to live in despair and
die prematurely.

Who is carrying whom in our economy? Who
creates the wealth that is so selfishly and divisively
guarded? No person can labor sufficiently to become

wealthy solely by his or her own labor. Our predation of the Earth's resources is openly visible and easily understood, but our individual, corporate, and social predation of the productive labor of others is masked through many laws, traditions, and political industrial conspiracies of economic domination protected by government police powers.

Socially, we want to control how our own labor is bartered, and have others do likewise. Economically, we want to own or control as much of other peoples labor as the rules of predation will allow; by employing others and making a profit from their labor. Politically, some want to change the rules to allow those who control vast amounts of labor, to control even more; while others wish to change the rules to prevent anyone from controlling vast amounts of labor. Social strife is ever present and change is slow.

The fundamental problem of economic predation, associated with the desire to amass and control great amounts of labor-money, is that for some to have more others must have less. If society is structured such that the productivity of our labor can be controlled and apportioned to allow some to amass vast labor-wealth, we need to understand that this can only occur at the expense of causing privation of labor goods and services and lack of opportunity for those at the bottom of the economic pyramid. We must also understand that the wealthy do not individually make themselves wealthy, and they do not individually maintain their wealth. The structure of society, and the control of that social structure, accomplishes the establishment and maintenance of wealth, and certainly the poverty that is required in order for relatively significant wealth to exist.

To understand how labor wealth is gathered and spent, consider a small community wherein certain persons labor a few hours a day to provide food, clothes, shelter, roads, schools, etc., for themselves. Everyone contributes and the workload is spread amongst those who can labor. If a ruler of this society decided that this community must furnish labor to build and maintain a castle for him, the community would have to allow certain people to give up their regular work and go and do these labors, which do not really benefit them or the community. The community labor diverted to this project would have to be made up by the remaining workers all working longer hours to provide the same level of goods and services as before, or the community would have to make do with fewer goods and services and suffer a reduced standard of living. The increased labor by the remaining community workers would be needed to feed, clothe and house those who must work for the ruler. If this community had 500 people working five hours each day, to produce goods to fulfill all of their needs, and half of them were forced to work on this project for the ruler, then the remaining workers would have to work ten hours each day to maintain the same level of community production and consumption. The required labor of the community has been greatly increased, but the consumption of goods and services by the average citizen has not increased. The ruler is able to control one-half of the productive labor of that community for his personal use and enjoyment, as well as to exclude all others from doing likewise.

Expand this situation to our whole society and it is easy to see why many must labor many hours a day and still live in poverty, so that others can labor very little and still live in affluence. Some must have less so that others can have more. Such a consequence can only occur through economic predation.

A wealthy person receives an income that may purchase hundreds, thousands, or millions of hours of other people's labor, in the form of goods and services, for only a few hours of their own time at work. Since we can only purchase labor products with surplus labor, those who control great amounts of labor and are able to purchase great amounts of products with the labor they control, may only do so by depriving other workers of the full value of their own productive labor. The predatory goal of wealth is to control labor and extract servitude from the working class to maintain the labor wealth provided by that servitude. Given the fantasies of wealth long in vogue in our society, it is not generally recognized that we cannot all live off the labor of others. In fact, if we wish to avoid debt, monetary as well as moral, we really have only our own productive labor upon which to depend.

For everyone to be wealthy at someone else's expense is impossible. For everyone to benefit fully from their own labor, being a burden to no one, and not being burdened by others, is Communist idealism and also impossible. Some must produce more, so that those who are unable to labor may be supported. Our social interactions create our economy, and our political interactions are supposed to channel our economic freedoms and responsibilities to create a general prosperity for everyone. The politicians are mismanaging our prosperity. Government cannot create prosperity; only our labors can do that. Government is meant to control how we deal with each other so that those who labor can have prosperity and security, and those who cannot labor should at least be able to share in the surplus. This has been perverted into the social principle that some must have less so that others can have more. When government channels prosperity towards those who have very much wealth in comparison to their labors, or in comparison to their share of communal responsibilities, it has perverted its purpose and prostituted its power.

We cannot all have butlers, maids, chauffeurs, gardeners and the like, simply because we do not have sufficient time to be all of those things for others. If a community of fifty men and fifty women decided that each man would have a valet and each woman would have a maid, then each man would have to be some other man's valet and each woman would have to be some other woman's maid. The problem with this society comes when one person wants to have a chauffeur as well as a valet or maid, causing some other person to give up having a valet or maid, so that the greedy one can have two servants. One cannot have more, unless someone else has less. Does this mean we should all have equal value for our labor? No! Those who have greater knowledge, skill, health, should receive proportionately less for the social value of their labor. It's the only way to get off this planet without accruing moral debts. Natural talents and luck do not guarantee a moral right to commit economic predation on the opportunities and products of others.

Societies can only operate on a social spectrum of two principles. On the one hand we have an "all for one and one for all" principle (fraternity), and on the other hand we have an "every person for their selves" principle (anarchy). Neither of these extremes requires established law to support itself, only commitment and non-commitment, respectively. While our great body of established law referees all of our social actions and alliances that fall in between fraternity and anarchy.

In general we disdain great personal labor, hoping for great wealth at other peoples' labor expense. But we are unwilling to equate this desire with the past perspective that held one race or one ethnic group as property of another race or ethnic group, subjugated economically and politically. Nor can we equate our desires for personal wealth with the past perspective that "common people" could be governed as if they were the property of kings and princes, to labor and bear economic and social burdens without representation or redress. This has allowed us to confuse ourselves into thinking that through our advances toward social liberty, we have somehow also gained or inherited some economic liberty. The concept of wealth, and the socially recognized right to acquire wealth at others labor expense, demonstrates our willingness to value labor and the economic liberty it can purchase, differently from social liberty. Therefore we allow labor to be apportioned differently. Though we pursue social liberty and social equality in a legal forum, we prevent them from ever being effectively implemented in society, because our economic structure is based on the lawful inequality of wealth and poverty (economic predation). The social equality of democracy will always be at odds with the economic inequality of capitalism, because the division of consumption does not follow the division of production (labor).

It is the social control of labor-profit that creates a society in which some may live in a Chateau de Brick, drink from crystal glasses, stay warm in winter and cool in summer, with fences to exclude others and police to enforce that exclusivity. While others live on a sidewalk, in a Chateau de Cardboard, with cold in the winter and heat in the summer, and in constant peril of losing their life, limbs, or meager possessions.

Freedom, or servitude; we thirst and strive for economic freedom, even at the social expense of causing others to serve us, and thereby lose some of their economic and social freedom. When we discuss the concept of involuntary servitude we most often think back in history of African slaves, indentured servants and prisoners sentenced to hard labor. Our modern societies are supported by involuntary servitude in two significant forms; namely, taxes and the prospect of a military draft. When the average worker must labor five months per year to pay the taxes exacted by our society, that worker is giving to society over 18-years of servitude in a 45-year working career. Though the preservation of society may demand an economic sacrifice or even demand service in the armed forces, being ordered into deadly combat without voice or choice; such sacrifices must be voluntary by assent and not coercion, if that society is to continue and prosper.

Relative wealth cannot exist without relative poverty, because they define each other. And both conditions have many members who consume the labor gathered from both our own working class, and from the working class of foreign societies, whose resources and labor have been controlled and exported here to serve the accumulation of wealth by our society. Such disparity continues, simply because economic classes create political classes, which are given to serving their benefactors by assuming lawful authority to control labor and access to resources. Since no country is one people indivisible, the world cannot be one people, indivisible. In capitalism we cannot all be equal and therefore it is a great fallacy of political thought that our economic system can generate or even tolerate equal opportunity or equal reward for equal labor. This may distress the romantics and liberals, but any effort to measure the different economic classes of our society, and the general lack of capacity for people to effect economic social change, will easily demonstrate the validity of this observation. It is only possible to create a society comprised of equal citizens with equal opportunity by treating all of them as mere cogs on a wheel, without individual talents or aspirations or authority; thereby denying them any freedom to act independently. Socialism has tried this and failed. Fraternity must be voluntary so that talents may be fully utilized. Equality of consumption is more important than any communistic attempt at equality of production.

The funds necessary to build and maintain our infrastructure, and thereby help maintain our prosperity, must come from taxes that are levied in such a manner that those who have most of the prosperity would also pay most of the taxes. It makes no sense to have a social structure that divides our society into classes that are continually at odds with each other, hoping to improve their prosperity at others' expense. The surplus labor we call capital ought to be protected by government when it preserves labor, and deals fairly with labor; otherwise it should be penalized by taxation to cover the social costs of its improprieties. If capital over-taxes labor to increase capital, then government must reduce taxes on labor and increase taxes on capital. If wealth is concentrated to the detriment of both economic and political security for the working class, then there should be additional taxes on wealth to re-establish economic and political security for everyone. Neither poverty nor lavish consumption should be tolerated.

In a very large economy it is difficult to see a direct connection between the labor of a farmer growing corn for animal feed, a factory worker building appliances, a teacher in a public school, a waitress in a restaurant, or a gardener on a private estate. All are producing something and all are consuming a variety of goods and services made available by our collective labors. But all of us are connected directly to each other's labor. Our national economy is a collective and so is our world economy. How we divide our collective labor, as far as consumption goes, masks the social web that binds us all together.

If we were asked to state our wage income from our jobs, we would answer with a dollar figure. Since we know that the dollars we spend are from our labor, and we realize, that for most of the goods we purchase, the labor cost to manufacture is well below the price we are required to pay; we commonly think our money does not represent a simple exchange of labor for labor. We need to understand that "Capital Welfare" is the taking of some productive labor from the manufacturing side and selling those goods for more than their labor cost (productive labor profit). The owners of industry operate in an economic environment of product control, which allows them to ask for more of your labor to purchase their goods for consumption, than was necessary to have those products made. And from the accumulation of this profit, paid in the form of the purchaser's labor, its owners and controllers can hire and support the labor necessary to provide them with the privilege of greater consumption.

If a person of wealth has more labor at their disposal than they can consume they simply use banks to loan it to others for the benefit of retrieving it for future consumption when the borrowers pay it back with future productive labor. The disparity of consumption, and the debts associated with the consumption of surplus goods and services are social issues that will not rectify themselves through actions of those who live at either the top or bottom of our economic pyramid. The workers support wealth-welfare and poverty-welfare, and until labor refuses to support this scheme it will continue to limit our social progress. The willingness to live in economic inequality will forever prevent social equality.

For those who do not or cannot labor productively, society must provide others to labor for them, to grow and transport food and clothing for them, to build homes for them, to provide medical care for them, and to educate them or their families. The secondary effect associated with providing goods and services to non-laborers is that those who labor exclusively to provide for the non-productive citizens must have other builders, farmers, physicians and teachers to provide for themselves and their families. To the degree that we are morally obligated to produce surpluses to provide for those who cannot provide for themselves, we are also morally obligated not to increase the number of people in this group. The greatest freedom that a society can offer all of its citizens is to provide goods and services for all without exaggerated deprivation or affluence, by requiring that all who can contribute will do so, and thereby minimize the amount of labor each person can be required to contribute to the support of others.

Consider a future situation in which all of our goods are manufactured, grown and transported by machines, with much of our infrastructure, such as buildings and highways, also made by robotic machines. These machines need only a few operators, and can also be repaired and maintained by other machines. If the people own these machines as a public corporation, then they may consume goods and services for the small labor of controlling the machines, and pursue other endeavors to enhance themselves and society. But if these machines are privately manufactured, or privately owned, then the manufacturers and owners will force the available labor of society to be diverted to their control, in exchange for the productivity of their machines. And if the owners of the machines likewise control the natural resources that the machines transform to sustain society, then those people unable to find jobs working for the machine owners would be left to live off the charity of the machine owners. While no one would needlessly starve, most would simply be maintained in relative poverty at a minimum resource expense. Labor barters for labor and those who are not allowed to labor can only be supported by charity or perish. While capitalism appears to reap the most benefits from technology, it also has the most to fear from technology. When people are removed from the productive labor and consumption loop by machines, they will have no allegiance to a social structure that permits private ownership to abandon un-needed laborers to become impoverished. Instead of enjoying the freedom from want that technology can provide, we will move toward social chaos.

The loss of jobs through technology has led to the near disappearance of the family farm and has contributed greatly to the decay of our cities. Highly productive farm machinery, fertilizers, and hybrid seeds have increased farm productivity such that the farm population in the U.S. has been reduced to 5% of our total population, down from 75% sixty years ago. Technology has also changed how and what we manufacture, such that thousands of manufacturing plants have closed or been moved overseas. The result has been high unemployment in our cities and the stranding of people in menial jobs or on welfare, with no real economic opportunities.

While technology has improved products and

created a multitude of new products, the biggest effect of technology has been to improve the efficiency of machines; requiring fewer people to operate machines, while producing more goods. The productivity of the American worker continues to rise, but this is not meant to indicate that his or her hands are moving faster and faster to produce more goods. We have been in the machine age for over one hundred years now, so our productivity increases in this century have to do with increased machine productivity. With computerization, machine productivity is rising rapidly today as compared with the past. Computers are replacing skilled laborers by being programmed to make the critical measurements of products as they are being made, and making judgments concerning the quality of products being produced by robotized machinery. The operators of those machines require less formal education and industrial training, allowing corporations to relocate manufacturing plants in countries where much lower wages, commensurate with lower skill requirements, are paid for equivalent work in the United States. And because the definition of increased productivity is more goods being produced at lower costs or with fewer man-hours, productivity only increases as relative wage costs decrease per item produced.

One segment of our society that had been nearly self-sufficient in the past, when simple manual labor was profitable, has now been rendered unproductive by technological change. That social group is housed in our prisons. How, on a planet that is obviously self-sufficient, can we have prisons that must operate at a great cost to society for their construction, maintenance and myriad provisions? Surely the period of incarceration for the mostly male population of our prisons can supply the necessary labor to build and maintain such prisons, as well as provide all of their food and clothes. The public should not have to contribute anything to the support of prisons, and should be able to expect the prison system to produce a surplus of material goods, whose sale could reimburse the victims of crime for their loss. As we reduce the amount of labor necessary to produce the goods and services we consume, we should transfer much of that labor requirement onto prisoners and those on probation for past crimes.

So is our society coming to an end? Perhaps; we cannot all be wealthy, we cannot all be criminals, or unemployed, or disabled, or on social welfare, or medical industry welfare, or defense industry welfare. Some must labor to provide a pool of surplus productive labor from which the non-laborers, or the medical establishment, or the defense establishment can draw their required goods and services. We have sufficient resources and labor capacity to maintain a healthy standard of living. The only requirement in our so-called free market is that we have an opportunity to labor, to be productive; for the express purpose of providing productive labor to spend for our own well being and to provide surplus labor for government to divide amongst those unable to labor.

Our economy is expanded by proper use of our collective surplus labor and capital, the sum total of which is called our Gross National Product. The apportioning of the GNP establishes our relative standards of living. If our GNP declines because of jobs moving out of the country, then we will have less surplus productive labor to tax to provide for our infrastructure and to share with those unable to labor. If the owners of the resources pay less and less for the labor necessary to manufacture the goods and services we consume, then government will not be able to tax the laborers to meet our communal needs. Government would then have to tax those owners to meet our communal shortfall or cut spending, regardless of the consequences.

Productivity and consumption go hand in hand. We all consume, and that which we consume is a portion of the world's gross production. The more of our productivity we are allowed to barter for our personal benefit, the more our individual standard of living is increased. The more our employers keep to enhance their standards of living, or the more government takes to disperse among the non-producing citizens to establish their standard of living, the more the laborer's standard of living is reduced. The same holds true with the whole world. Some nations have less control over their resources and productive labor, so that other nations may have more. The optimum labor situation world-wide is one where each person is able and has ample opportunity to labor for his or her own benefit, contributing only to close family and community infrastructure. Then each person would have a high standard of living or a greatly reduced labor requirement, a choice they could make for themselves. But labor opportunity throughout the world is not optimum, nor is it easy to see exactly what is fair and what is oppressive. Within nations and between nations we are unwilling to recognize the equivalence of labor, hour for hour worldwide. The superior knowledge and skill of one society can be put to the use and betterment of all, or it can be perverted toward economic colonization, for the purpose of extracting resources and disparaged labor. Generations of this type of oppression lead to the establishing of different classes throughout the world in regard to standards of living.

In an isolated economy we would expect wages and prices to stabilize and to a great extent equalize, with production varying to meet demand; and opportunity to labor shared by all who can labor such that the hours needed to produce goods would also be equally shared by all workers. Or we would expect wages to decline steadily and continuously, until the laborers were working extremely long hours for subsistence wages. This would be the result of an economic system that requires workers to compete for an opportunity to labor; with many workers unemployed being the leverage against wage increases for those with jobs. The difference in the direction an economy takes is tied to resource ownership and the moral philosophy, or lack thereof, of those who control the resources and control the labor that transforms them. In the real world, especially Second- and Third-World countries, we have seen laborers forced to work longer and longer hours for money that has less and less trade value. We have heard reports of high inflation figures coming out of South America and other continents without realizing that we and other First-World economies are in concert with the elitist class of owners in these countries, sucking the well dry of labor and resources. In the Third-World a person may labor twelve to sixteen hours a day, and still be unable to take care of his or her family. The spouse may need to find work also, and if that is not enough, the children may need to abandon school and a meaningful future to strive along side their parents. There is something grossly out of balance in that economy and the relationship between owners, laborers and foreign consumers. Only when there is insufficient opportunity and reward for labor, do we have famines such as are happening in Africa, or decades of inflationary duress such as has been occurring in South America. The first types of decay that anticipate these foreign disasters are upon us. The average family is working longer hours to make ends meet. The federal government, which used to fund all sorts of social programs, contributed to many state programs which aided the elderly, the poor, the handicapped, the abused and the disabled, is continually cutting or abolishing these programs. The federal government needs those dollars to pay the wealthy more and more interest on the debt that they are so gracious to continue financing. The increase in poverty, misery, illiteracy, homelessness and rampant crime can be laid directly and specifically at the feet of the debt financiers and their political minions.

As a society we continually talk about wanting to do more and more to support those who are unemployed, or disadvantaged in some other manner. But in our economy we allow and even encourage companies to profit from disparaged labor, believing that society as a whole should care and contribute, while corporate greed should be free to pursue profit. If economies run in cycles of full employment in some years, and significant unemployment in other years, then where is government in the good years when something needs to be set aside for the bad years; a time when many companies are operating with reduced profits, or even deficits? In what manner can something be set-aside for the lean years? Is being middle class an economic contract that can be canceled like a job? Or is the middle class a socio-economic class that may pursue economic survival via the political processes of abrogating debts and asset protection for the wealthy? Under the democratic principle that we are one people, and should sink or swim together. Do we have a representative democracy to enact laws for the benefit of all, or do we just have a representative democracy to

40

elect the enactors, who become the servants of the wealthy and the taskmasters of the workers and wardens of the poor?

The desire to expand production requires the expansion of the producing class. Reducing taxes and some services to the poor and increasing taxes on the wealthy could best accomplish this. Which would then decrease the community burden on the middle class, and allow them to barter their surplus labor with each other, thereby offering opportunities to expand the middle class by employing and educating the poor. The idle rich might also be drawn back into the labor class. The higher the taxes on the surplus income of those who are not proportionately productive in our society, the greater the benefit towards providing a better infrastructure for all. We cannot have recessions and depressions if we have access to resources and the opportunity to labor. But without these, we could have tremendous economic deprivation, even in a world of abundant resources and capacity to labor.

The definition of industrialization is the use of energized machines to make goods without our specific "hand-made" labor. To avoid economic social strife we need to focus on technology as a means to liberate everyone from poverty, reduce everyone's daily hours of labor, and develop a world-wide consensus of what a minimum standard of living should be, guaranteed through international treaties and the transfer of sustaining technology and resources. Society must own and control the use of technology, or the owners of technology will control society.

If our wealth is dependent upon our productivity, then what is being done in America to maintain our high production capacity? For years we were able to lead the world in manufacturing and consumption through inventive technology, and ever increasing use of machines with greater and greater production capacities. We were also able to pay the labor costs of building and maintaining our infrastructure, and all the other costs associated with government. With the expanding free trade agreements, as well as the social-political awakenings worldwide, it is probable that the productivity of foreign labor will not be as readily available to be siphoned off to feed our economy.

Rather, foreign productivity will begin competing with our factories and farms to provide finished goods to us as consumers, resulting in a labor-profit to themselves and a jobs-lost detriment to ourselves. In the past when we lost jobs to technology we at least increased productivity, which reduced the relative cost of those goods. This has the effect of enriching those who consume these cheaper goods, allowing them to spend additional labor-dollars in other areas of the economy, which in turn has the effect of increasing production of other goods and job opportunities.

It is one thing to build a factory within a society to make goods for that society to consume; exporting a portion of their surplus production to other smaller societies that cannot afford to build such factories. It is quite another thing to build a factory in a country that consumes virtually none of the goods produced there; exporting those goods to wealthier societies with the sole purpose of milking them of some of their labor-wealth, causing job loss, tax loss and eventually poverty for laid-off workers. Allowing corporations to be multi-national, having no allegiance to any society but their stockholders encourages them to locate anywhere and oppress any society that can provide a cheap labor base, as well as low taxes on profits. They move their cheaper goods into consuming economies, hurting the companies and workers who operate in a higher wage and tax environment by pressuring those companies to lower wages to compete or loose market-share and have to layoff workers. Exporting jobs to other countries means importing poverty here. We have seen this system of economic predation at work for a few hundred years now. Is it necessary to allow multi-national corporations to destroy our economy through multi-national profiteering, or just fitting retribution for our past dominance and predation of many foreign economies?

If we consider that without profits, and the search for ever-greater profits from investments and ownership, we would all have to labor productively, to fulfill our own needs. And whether we labored competitively, or fraternally, we would come to view our labors as relatively equivalent. In a moral sense we may suppose that an hour of labor in any given task is equivalent in value to an hour of labor given to any other task. However, in our current marketplace, it is not the time expended, but rather the amount of goods produced in a given time, that determines labor value. So increased productivity is the goal of profit-based economies, and the inspiration for many inventions.

Overall in our economy, the gain in productivity through technical advances does not offset the loss of opportunity to the families of those who were laid off from work due to newer technology. After all, industry would not invest in new technology that would increase productivity unless there were a savings in labor cost which would be greater than the cost of that technology. Our industries are gaining increased productivity, because of the elimination of manufacturing jobs by machines that have several times the productivity of one laborer. This is all well and good if that higher productivity means higher taxes to care for those newly unemployed. Since unemployment is only partially paid by the employers, our workers are forced to support the long term unemployed in a welfare format, while stockholders reap potentially greater rewards. The creation of unemployment for the purpose of corporate economic gain pits the anarchy of capitalism against the social communism of democracy. Such is the failure of the "division of labor" principle, because it is subordinated to a perverted division of consumption. Inventive technology requires an increase in economic predation (profit) or it will cease searching for greater efficiencies of production regardless of social needs.

Consider an early community where houses and buildings were made from clay bricks, and a few men were working independently in the available clay pits to supply the needs of their community. In a general sense the laborers in each pit shared the free resource clay, and they shared the community's demand for bricks. They were able to barter their brick-making labor to have a standard of living similar to the other members of that society. Until some enterprising person built a machine to produce more bricks with just one person's labor, than the efforts of the other laborers in that pit combined. Rather than share this technology, he claimed ownership of the machine and its production, which now allowed him to prey on his fellow workers and all of the citizens in that community. This person proposed to the other workers in one clay pit that he could produce enough bricks to give each of them half of their regular production each day, if they would allow him to control the use of clay in that pit. This would allow them to pursue other labor opportunities, and still have some bricks to barter in the community. Essentially these newly unemployed brick makers had become stockholders in this private enterprise venture and for the time being had a somewhat higher standard of living than those who did not profit from the machine's labor.

With the production capacity of his machine, and control of the clay in this pit, the entrepreneur was able to amass many bricks in a stockpile, which were temporarily used to lower the cost of bricks to the consumers of bricks. This caused a drop in the income and therefore a drop in the standard of living of brick makers in all of the local clay pits. When it became difficult to make a living as a brick maker many sought other work, abandoning their clay pits. Others became employees of the entrepreneur. The entrepreneur then used his profits to purchase the right to control all of the available clay pits, to promote a supposed social harmony and control of labor opportunities. Although bricks were still available to the community, these clay pits became non-existent to the community, because his ownership kept them from having free access to that part of the Earth.

Through total control of the resource, he was then able to establish a high trading value for his bricks, guarding only against some other building material becoming cheaper. With the productivity of his machine, as well as the control of labor still needed to operate the machine and transport bricks to market, he was able to barter that productivity to gain ownership of other resources. At which point the whole community became his employees, and were beholden to him for their very existence and standard of living. They had become economic and political slaves and he had become the owner of all resources, and therefore King. He controlled all their opportunities for education, employment, medical care, and old age pensions. Where the community labored with the environment to produce useful goods, he labored to control their access to technology, resources and their access to markets where they could trade their labor-goods. Such is pure economic predation.

This is how monarchies have operated down through the ages. The rulers subjugated the people, both economically and politically, in that they could not own land or resources. Since politics is subordinate to economics, the workers had no political rights because they had no economic rights. Their labor was continually taken to support the military ambitions of their overseers, or to support the administrative aristocracy in the social pyramids of society. This type of social structure was one of control and persecution, not defense of liberty.

The social miracle of inventive technology is that if it is put to use for community benefit it lightens the burdens associated with its creation, freeing all persons to pursue greater knowledge and additional inventions. If society owns the right to control how discoveries are put to use, the loss of employment by technology would be of great benefit to society. Because it would free workers to apply their labors in other areas of the economy wherever it would benefit them and their society the most. However, if that inventive technology is privately owned, and used to acquire the communities' surplus labor, it becomes a social disease that corners resources, limits opportunity, perverts politics and foments social unrest. The result is a society that permits the private control of commodities even to a point of withholding goods to extract windfall profits, or which allows the purchase of technology for the express purpose of reducing jobs. For those able to labor, our society demands that we support ourselves with our own labor, or suffer the consequences of an uncaring and uncharitable competitive economy, while industry is encouraged if not required by stockholders and speculators to always maximize profits regardless of the social consequences. If all things can be provided by machines that require little or no control by workers, then there will be no opportunities to labor and barter that labor amongst ourselves. Societies will both become the owner of that technology and bring with it a new social order, or we will not have societies.

The reason for cornering the market on clay in our

model community was because of the value it had in exchange for other people's labor. That value was determined by want and need bartering for the available supply. If something else, such as ready-mix concrete, had been available, the clay pits would have been abandoned and deemed worthless. So although it appears that the clay pits as property and as a resource had a money value, what they actually had was a labor exchange value, determined by the current willingness of consumers to exchange their productive labor for clay bricks, and a prediction of future demand based on that current demand. Such are the values of all property and resources. No present demand and no future demand, means no exchange, and therefore no economic value. Equally important for all societies, no skilled labor force or operating factories means no domestic labor to exchange, creating a situation where domestic resources will be exported to other societies to only benefit the owners of those resources.

Resource ownership exists to control and profit from labor, and all of the ingenious goods that are forthcoming from labor; it does not matter to the resource owners if that labor is foreign or domestic. In and of itself, a labor value attached to property and resources is not socially immoral. But the degree to which resources are withheld or controlled by monopoly, especially when lives and future generations are at stake, has become the social hammer that is forging new views on private property and world-wide resources. The market economies have operated for hundreds of years under the notion that greater demand for a resource should automatically cause the bartering value of that resource to rise until demand is reduced to equal the available supply. In such a system, those without surplus labor to trade are completely ignored. Only labor is recognized, and only labor can establish a demand for resources and other labor. While charity may be of social or political benefit, it is not of economic benefit.

We are deceived that our economy is a free market, and that the politicians will make laws to protect the free market concept. In reality, we have never had a free market, or a conspiratorial military-industrial complex. We have always had a disguised and conspiratorial, political-industrial complex, controlling the economy. Its elected minions in Washington conspire to control the labor wealth of our economy, as well as other economies world-wide, to the benefit of their patrons and benefactors, making sure that it will never be a free market. The nations' capital can be moved, by its owners, to any economy on the planet that offers greater opportunities for that capital to be increased, regardless of the economic oppression or decay it may cause. Even the military may be used, and disposed to serve the elite under the contemporary wags of patriotism. The military is an extension of political will, and political will is an extension of the economic will that controls economic opportunity.

This book is not revelation; these insights are known to many. Those who believe in social and economic equality, or equality of opportunity, may believe that society simply does not understand how it is structured, or how that structure can be changed. But I submit that we know how and why society is structured like it is. We are not 300-million Americans marching side by side, fighting the foes of Liberty, as brothers and sisters of equality. Power knows its power, and chooses its persecution. Many who have economic and political power do by choice subvert and pervert our system of laws to gain advantage and preservation of their interests over and above others, without regard to social consequences. There is a historical philosophy of power that whoever is on top rules, and fights to preserve their rule. This is recognition that we cannot all be in a position to rule and to reap the political benefits of economic power. It is not true that those who control the economy and reap the rewards of ownership are ignorant of their position, or are willing to promote true social and economic equality.

It is not likely that societies can free themselves of corruption, or can return themselves to domestic tranquility when economic unrest is prevalent, without an attempt to re-distribute the resource-wealth and social obligations of the different economic classes; most likely an unpleasant undertaking. So let's dispense with the notion of money as something separate from someone's labor, and realize where our wealth comes from. At least we would have a baseline from which to measure our collective wealth, and our ability to maintain and or expand that wealth in the future. Likewise, it would give us the ability to focus on the social requirements necessary to thwart a decline in our ability as a nation to continue providing to ourselves the fruits of our labor. We must limit and control our social and economic predation of our societies as well as our earthly resources.

Chapter 3 - Ownership and Monopoly

There are two extreme ways that surplus labor may be dispersed in a society. One is to have each worker keep all of his or her productive labor for themselves, and to barter it as they see fit, without regard to community needs or charity (zero charity and taxes). The other extreme is for the governing body to receive all goods from their producers, free of obligation to those workers, and to disperse goods, services, lands and habitations to those who are in need or who have a skill that can transform resources to provide future surplus goods (100% taxation). There are numerous ways to control the distribution of goods and services in between the two extremes. Our current social tax system operates somewhere in the middle.

Two concepts, which are as closely related as the sides of a coin, are missing from our above examples of economic interaction; they are ownership and debt. Ownership in our society means a socially recognized right to control land, resources and the products of our labor, for the personal profit and benefit of the owners. Whenever land and resources are owned in a manner that is not community based, ownership may deny access to land or resources. The compilation of hundreds of years of written law protects the social right of ownership (private property), and insists it is an inalienable right. Debt cannot exist, in the socio-economic sense, without private ownership of resources and the exchange of those resources for our surplus labor, stored labor or the promise of payment of future labor. Social classes, disparity of income, denial of opportunity, untreated disease, mal-nutrition, starvation, in the midst of peace and plenty, all arise from ownership and debt.

We obligate our future labor to owners when we borrow from the surplus they control to satisfy our daily needs. We must give our labor to the owners of the land and resources in order to sustain ourselves. We perish when our labor is not needed and owners will not allow us to labor to obtain goods and services to sustain ourselves. This is as true for nations as it is for individuals, and has been the source of much war and conflict. Certainly throughout history there have been some forms of ownership and debt in the most altruistic communities. Likewise, there have been some social controls and charity in the most anarchistic societies. A more in-depth look at debt and ownership in our contemporary society will help explain our declining civilization.

In common understanding the term - Land - refers simply to a piece of ground, solid earth. In economic concepts, land is everything, not only the solid earth, but every animal and vegetable upon the Earth, every lake, river and ocean, all animals that swim or fly as well as walk, and all minerals that can be dug out of the Earth. All are part of the "LAND." Even people are, and have been at all times in the past, a slave commodity, bought, sold and controlled to provide labor for the harvesting of the "land." Most people are still part of the "land", and not free.

To the degree that the solid earth is owned privately instead of publicly, that resources are owned exclusively instead of inclusively, that nations structure their laws to be exclusive rather than inclusive, is the degree to which war will continue to destroy and re-distribute ownership of the "land." War is perpetual on Earth because ignorance, selfishness, greed and lust for power over the "land" are ingrained in all peoples by historical precedent.

Though the world has different laws and customs to permit ownership of property and resources, western capitalism is becoming the dominant economic, and therefore political, manner of controlling "land."

When one person or corporation pays to purchase resources or raw materials, they are not really paying for the materials themselves, the resources are free; they are simply part of the earth. What they are paying for is the socially recognized protection system of resource control, which allows them to bring their purchased resources into our economies and barter them for the labor of those who choose to consume those resources. The exchange of surplus labor today, to control a resource to harvest future labor, is the foundation of our social property rights laws. That ownership allows a complete monopoly over the use or non-use of resources, (trespassers will be incarcerated). For example, if the socially recognized owners of trees live in an economic climate wherein few trees are consumed, they would find the labor value of their resource reduced to a point where they may have to abandon ownership of trees, and suffer the loss of the surplus labor they paid to control that resource. On the other hand, we presently imprison people who steal trees from the forest, because they are taking something for which another party had the exclusive right to control.

Ownership, and the social protections that permit and promote ownership, is the foundation of our capitalist system. Workers, trying to barter their labor for products or services of other workers' labor, must pay a labor premium which we call profit to the owners of the goods and services that they purchase and consume. When you pay two hours labor for goods that cost only one hour of manufacturing, transporting and sales clerk time to provide it to the consumer, then you are giving that extra hour of your labor as profit to the owners of the factory and transportation company and retail company. This labor profit is just one way that owners are able to amass a great amount of your labor, to barter for goods and services to their exclusive benefit, or to purchase exclusive control of additional resources.

If an owner of a factory sells goods for twice the labor cost to manufacture them, then that owner could receive two million hours of productive labor from consumers and only have to give one million hours of that labor to his employees as wages. The owner would then have one million hours of his factory's productive labor to barter for the community labor that will build a mansion and a vacation home, purchase greater police protection and legal representation, and provide his children with better education and opportunities to take over and maintain such ownership relationships. If our factory owner cannot consume all of the labor available to him, he may choose to lend some surplus labor to others to consume today, if he is sure he will be repaid with even more labor than he lends. He can take advantage of want or need, postpone the consumption of his acquired surplus labor, and receive a greater return on his surplus labor wealth in the future. Year after year, and even generation after generation, the increasing surplus repaid to an owner from loans can only be used to purchase goods and services, more lands and resources, or be loaned again. It must be used to consume goods and services, directly or through loans, or it does not exist.

Debt can only come about when there is a surplus to borrow from and when someone who owns and controls a surplus is willing to lend. Rather than distributing today's surpluses amongst would-be consumers, without obligation to repay, our society allows owners to lend surpluses to others. Since the repayment of debt can only be made from future surplus labor, if you do not have a job lenders will refuse to allow you to borrow their surplus goods. Those unable to labor may live in privation, while goods sufficient to sustain them are readily available. Such privation occurs continually in some parts of the world. Almost all countries have some part of their population living in unnecessary privation. While laborers go into debt to consume the very surplus that they produce with their labors.

If a surplus of goods exists, over and above current cash demand, then two options are available to increase consumption. One is to lower prices so that more cash sales will occur, under the economic rule that if supply exceeds demand, prices must fall until additional demand consumes that surplus. The other option is to keep prices high and contract with would-be consumers to let them receive goods from owners now and pay for them over time with future labor-money. This not only keeps prices higher than they should be, it disguises the true economic strength of the workers by allowing the government to count debt transactions as cash transactions when they occur, rather than when payments are made. Take a community in which ten more houses sold this month than last, for an average cost of $400,000 dollars each. The total economic activity in that community has not increased by four million dollars; it has only increased by any fees and down payments actually paid on those houses. That four-million-dollar commitment plus interest is based on presumed future economic activity, not current or past economic activity. Similarly, all credit purchases are not a gauge of current economic activity, and debt certainly does not guarantee a robust economy in the future. Rather it is a drag on the economy.

In a social economy operated to produce goods and services for the needs of all members, there would be no debt, no selling for profit, no over-production, or competition to control consumption. Labor would exchange for labor in a purely cash economy. In our present economy production is not controlled to fulfill consumption demands, but rather to control those demands to produce debt amongst consumers, in order to gain control over those consumers' future labor. Debt provides larger profits for employers today, as well as ongoing pressure to keep wages down, because workers in debt must be certain of future income to pay their debts and therefore are more productive to protect their employment and less likely to seek pay increases that might price them out of a job. Debt consumption is an immoral usury of the free resources given to all that are born on Earth. It results in economic oppression, if not slavery, for the majority of peoples.

If surplus goods are sold on debt contracts (any form of credit), debtors will not be available to purchase additional surplus goods unless they pay off that debt, or incur more debt. Continued over-production ultimately exhausts credit-worthy purchasers. Unless more and more credit is extended, further and further into the future, obligating more and more future labor to pay for today's consumption, the economy will exhaust the credit that it can issue and have to operate as if it were solely a cash and carry economy.

Society is not increasing its standard of living by extending credit further into the future, to the contrary, it is decreasing its ability to sustain today's standard of living; by obligating future income to pay for today's goods and services that will decay or wear out or become obsolete before the consumer's debt is paid. Government errs greatly when it encourages or allows certain types of debt, because it encourages people to consume beyond their means, and allows owners to reap future obligations far beyond their needs. The extension of credit creates a false standard of living, which can be undone by economic depression when credit is not available. When credit evaporates, desperate manufacturers will devalue our productive labor to sell their goods at any price, trying to keep their companies going amid declining consumption. Tens of millions of jobs can be terminated, further undermining consumption. In our economy, the means to consume is always placed ahead of the need to consume.

Much of the established wealth in our society (old money) comes from the ownership of real estate. Old money receives its income by renting or leasing industrial properties, office buildings, apartment buildings, etc. As long as demand is maintained or increased, all taxes and maintenance costs are passed along to the renters and leaseholders. The money paid to landlords is surplus labor from the productive parts of our society. Like other welfare recipients, landlords need labor money in order to purchase in the marketplace the goods and services necessary to live. All persons who do not labor to produce the goods and services consumed in our society must obtain theirs by receiving welfare from taxation, or rents and leases of land, or sales of raw materials out of the ground, or as owners of factories.

Although our nation was politically unique, some two hundred years ago; Europe still controlled our economy. The hereditary and social monopoly of European economies was in place in the American Colonies, which had strong trade ties to Europe. But the Revolutionary War and the establishing of the US Constitution, along with a policy to displace the native peoples through a government power of eminent domain, to take land and disburse it amongst a growing immigrant population, allowed us to avoid developing Europe's rigid social classes.

The American Colonies flourished because of an abundance of resources, labor and room to expand. The founders of our government already had a functioning economy based on the concept of private property. And they had social inequality based on ownership prior to our independence. Any who chose could go west and become owners and exploiters, without the potential for great conflict with already established businesses and communities. Laws were designed to protect and nurture this economic system of expansion. But we have now run out of people and places to exploit. We are now faced with social conflict with those who have labor or resources that we would like to consume. We must change our economies and social systems or face social revolts against the exploitation that is the cause of such conflicts.

The principle power associated with ownership of land, resources, manufacturing plants, patents on ideas and products, copyrights on intellectual products, is the power of monopoly. Monopoly is exclusive control of the means of production and the surplus labor gathered from profits on production.

Obviously the Earth is a finite size, and though we have not analyzed and catalogued its entire surface to know how much of its many resources are available for consumption, we have already divided, apportioned and restricted access to most resources through government and corporate monopoly. The first level of monopoly is national; each nation establishes laws, taxes, and tariffs to exercise some control and profit over the distribution and consumption of its natural resources. Within many nations, national and international corporations purchase control over some resources, and then attempt to monopolize the consumption of such resources for their maximum profit. In many cases resources are bought and kept off the world market to reduce supply and thereby maintain higher prices. When this is done it is as if the Earth has been reduced in size and capacity, while competition is thwarted, to enrich those holding such monopolies. Some monopolies are even destructive of our social existence, as for example, international oil companies buying up patents on fuel formulas, efficiency devices, and even competing technologies such as solar energy and super-conductors, to keep these technologies undeveloped and their oil consumed at a high volume and cost. They benefit from your spending more of your labor to consume their monopolized resources.

Monopolies are not necessarily national or international. Most monopolies are regional or even community based. If there is only one electric utility company in your community, it is a monopoly and is usually government regulated. Even the local pizza parlor and dry cleaner are local monopolies, maintained by their convenience to a particular neighborhood and controlled by the distance to their competitors; the greater the distance to a competitor, the greater the freedom to monopolize local demand for goods or services. Several small monopolies in a community may not appear to inhibit the local economy. But any unregulated monopoly will adversely affect the health and growth of other companies by receiving more labor for its goods or services than would be exchanged in a competitive market. Since there is a finite amount of surplus labor and resources in any community, more for one is less for others.

To own a small piece of land, even to just have a home and yard on it, is the right to monopolize what activities may take place there, the right to say who may come or who may not trespass. This right is extended to all private lands and resources. Landowners may sell or not sell their trees, minerals or other items of social value.

In manufacturing, monopolies exist such that the owners decide what will be made, where it will be made, who will be hired to make it, and how much will be made, depending on demand and whether the monopoly is only partial or complete. The class structure of our society (owners, laborers and the indigent) is founded in the power of ownership and monopoly, because political power is subservient to economic power, creating a legal structure that promotes the maintenance of ownership and monopolies over our lands and resources and opportunities.

It is only through political and economic monopolies that a country like the U.S. could lead the world in technology, produce an abundance of goods and services for all, and have such a disparity of wealth and opportunity. The monopolizing of labor causes us to abandon those not able to labor, into a life of poverty supported by so-called charity and government welfare aide. It is oppression, not charity, to give people subsistence in order to monopolize opportunity.

There is a huge difference between entrepreneurial capital (intellectual talent) and historical capital (stored labor). The right of ownership of ideas and inventive genius to produce improved or new products is certainly responsible for our historic leap through the industrial age, into the high-tech age. But such ownership can lead to monopolies that may disrupt many other lives in the labor market as new technology renders some labor as unnecessary and diverts other labor as profit to the inventors. Many inventions and innovations are often sold to manufacturers who then control such products to produce a monopoly for purely economic gain. Such benefit of monopolies to help one company comes directly out of the cost to consumers and the cost for other companies to compete. Technology often displaces labor, which continually disrupts many lives, placing a burden on society that is not compensated.

Probably the most disparaging monopolies are in the medical-pharmaceutical industry. Where many innovative procedures, high-tech diagnosis equipment, and new or improved medicines are made available, through monopoly control, at prices that are well above an average individual's ability to pay. Our medical insurance, which initially spread the risk of cost for medical care, is now the cash cow for many companies in the medical industry. Their patents allow them to charge more than the market can bear, forcing insurance companies and Medicare-Medicaid safety nets to raise premiums and taxes to feed those monopolies. While simultaneously degrading the care that physicians and hospitals may provide to keep costs in line. It is ironic that such industries make such huge profits on personal misery, while morality teaches us that is a grave sin to profit from the misery of others. After all, we are all going together or we are not going at all.

The ability through ownership to monopolize land, resources and technology and the ability to transfer that ownership are a continual source of social oppression. Monopolies may lead to the anarchy that results when mergers and acquisitions further reduce the number of competitors, allowing prices and production to control consumption rather than the other way round. Without competition, surplus labor can be directed toward controlling more land and resources to discourage competition, rather than contributed to society through lower prices or the advancement of technology. Competition serves all of society by allowing consumer demand to control the price and quality of goods.

The fundamental purpose of our political system is the establishment and preservation of our economic system. Political power subordinates to economic power by definition and design. Socio-economic power resides in resource and labor control, and politics cannot determine who will have that power. The feudal lords of Europe claimed ownership of lands and resources, far and near. They were able to do so because of the power of their militaries to force all other people to accept and respect those economic claims. Today, we have substituted more representative forms of government in our societies, and given them power to promote more equitable forms of economic interaction. Still, we are stuck with disproportionate ownership of labor, land and resources, because of disproportionate control of political power. The police and the military organizations of a country serve to preserve the political systems that empower them. Which is to say, they preserve the economic systems that control the political systems that oversee the police and military. We are in error when we assume that we may control political power over and above our economic power. And we commit an even greater error when we believe that political power is the supreme power in our societies. The greatest power is control of the "land." Through its control, all labor opportunities and wages are controlled. Division of labor is established, overall productivity is controlled to produce only certain goods in limited quantities, to facilitate a division of consumption that disparages the majority of all people. Such controls are always economic issues before they are political issues. This is demonstrated in any country where the military has overthrown a political system that was out of favor with the wealthy elite. Haiti and Argentina are good examples of a past military administration running a social system for the well to do, when the politicians failed to realize their place in the hierarchy of economic and political power.

Chapter 4 - Capitalism and the Economic Pyramid

The individual laborer is sustained by his or her productive labor, but society is created and sustained by his and her surplus productive labor. We create surpluses for future consumption, but we control them in the sense of who may distribute those surpluses to their exclusive benefit, and then we call such surpluses "wealth". When those surpluses are used to expand the productive economy, they are called "capital." The use of private wealth (surpluses) to build and control industries is the foundation of Capitalism.

Capitalism is used to generate a pool of surplus labor stored in goods, infrastructure and consumption debt. Our democracy is supposed to regulate the distribution of that surplus labor. But our political system has been subordinated to the power of wealth from its beginning. Capitalism, unchecked by social examination and regulation, and unguided by principles of liberty and relative equality of opportunity, will tend toward what we call oligarchy; where a few hold power to rule and perpetuate their rule by economic and political tyranny. Voters have little recourse to correct the actions of an oligarchy, because political parties, which are controlled by the oligarchy, choose the candidates.

Through capitalism we are forced to build an economic pyramid, arising from a foundation of economic inequality, and then we consume our social energies trying to politically re-arrange it. However we may arrange it, our pyramid requires that many must be at the bottom so that a few can be at the top. Those at the top of our socio-economic pyramid continually delude the poor and middle class into believing that all of us could join them if we simply work harder.

In the past, society was also structured like a pyramid. A king or queen stood at the top, aristocracy further down, merchants further down, and serfs and slaves at the bottom. Societies were quite rigid then, in that one could not easily change classes, regardless of their abilities. In today's pyramid, fate, violence, corruption, or the right connections, can allow anyone to obtain any position in our pyramid. The opportunities of ownership and control that are available to some can only occur if those same opportunities are denied others. The unemployed are left milling about near the pyramid, hoping for an opportunity to join the structure and work for or inherit a place at the top. The pyramidal axiom of capitalism is; "some must labor more and receive less so that others may labor less and receive more". Though our modern economic pyramid is more fluid in the sense that your class at birth does not now prohibit you from rising higher in that pyramid, our economic structure will always require that many must labor and receive less to support a few who will receive more.

America may be the land of opportunity, but it is not the land of equal opportunity. By limiting access to education, especially higher education, we create a pyramid of individual capacity that interfaces with our economic pyramid of ownership and productive labor. Rather than discipline children to learn and attain certain skill levels before advancement in primary and secondary schools, we matriculate all children according to their age. Such measures only create classes that are peers in age, not in ability. This does not profit the majority of students; it only supplies our economy with new replacements for those retiring from our economic pyramid. We do not want the majority to be peers in capacity. We want many to be very limited in skills, willing to do as they are told for wages that do not permit any opportunity to acquire surplus labor and economic independence.

The anarchy of the capitalistic marketplace is always searching for increases in efficiency and more resources. Through technology we are able to increase industrial production and to locate or extract more resources from the Earth. Technology continually improves productivity because of competition for increased profits. But competition can be both constructive and destructive. Constructive competition promotes increased technology and frees up labor to pursue the production of more and varied products, conserving resources and reducing the labor input of society while raising the over-all standard of living for all. On the other hand competition often allows one person or company to control sufficient resources to destroy its competitors by temporary over-supply of its goods, and lowering prices below production cost; using its stored labor-capital to carry it until its competitors go out of business. Those who are driven out of business and into unemployment will have to be carried by the rest of the laboring economy. The company that is victorious in such an economic battle will then have a greater monopoly over the consumption of its goods or services. This will lead to price increases, which will ignore need. Those without sufficient labor-money to exchange will be unable to consume.

Regardless of the strength or weakness of any company in our economy, all companies should be required to make a profit on current sales to moderate competition. And all companies, regardless of profits should pay a percentage tax on gross sales.

Government should have the authority to liberate resources that are being monopolized, and further, to support companies whose growth will foster good competition. Doing this within the nation, and as a nation competing with other nations, would bring the world into an economic system wherein all standards of living would tend to equalize; needed goods and services should be produced in sufficient quantity to meet demand, and their prices regulated if necessary. But an equal reward for equal labor is equal consumption, nearly impossible to establish and control. Inequality establishes itself easily, responding only partially and grudgingly to social controls. Ownership and monopoly are the antithesis of economic freedom and will forever deny such freedom.

A capitalist economy must always increase productivity with machine technology that reduces the need for human labor, rather than use technology to increase overall company productivity to produce and sell more goods at a lower price. It's apparently irrational to believe that auto makers should work together world-wide to meet the transportation needs of all economies, and do it for lower and lower costs as technology reduces the labor needed to manufacture those cars. Consumers should benefit from such price reductions without having to bear the increased burden of supporting those who become unemployed. Social freedom and harmony would be more forthcoming if technology was universally shared.

Surplus Labor is our only source of capital. When our government talks of tax policies that promote the creation of capital, or which promote capital investments, the government is really just talking about surplus labor. This surplus labor can be the potential of machines and materials to build things (stored labor). It can be what we call borrowed capital (current surplus), debt acquired in order to build or expand a business. In either case, the recent focus of the government has been to aid the wealthy in gathering more and more capital, which has been poorly invested and scandalously misused. We have for most of the last generation been borrowing from the wealthy, the surplus labor they have taken from workers, to finance government deficits; requiring future workers to repay the wealthy for the communal use of today's surplus labor.

The wealthy of today are so ignorant of how capital must be generated and expended to promote social stability that they invest and build to undo each other. One corporation moves outside the country to reduce its labor costs, causing unemployment here. Its competitors point to that event and force labor unions to give back wages and benefits. Still other industries see these tactics and do likewise. This may generate more profits for some corporations temporarily, but when the laborer receives less and less of his or her own labor to barter for goods and services; they obviously spend less, which hurts all manners of industries. Too much pressure on labor from the wealthy or from government will cause a downward spiral of economic activity, and an explosion of debt that cannot be repaid; resulting in a long economic depression.

Rather than lower capital gains taxes to promote resource availability, we can encourage the wealthy of our country to invest in our economy in times of economic decline by increasing their income taxes and capital gains taxes on a sliding scale, averaging 1% or 2% more tax for every 1/10% increase in unemployment and or every 1/10% increase in welfare recipients. We should set a benchmark of 4% unemployment and 5% welfare recipients, and begin with those whose personal income is in excess of $125,000 annually. This along with a law to limit dividends, interest receipts, and capital gains on investment outside our country when unemployment rises above 4%, will force the wealthy to turn over resource assets both to meet increasing tax burdens on their income, and to get the economy rolling again, and have their taxes reduced. If the capitalists believe that only the wealthy can lead us out of recessions and depressions, then we can persuade them to do so by threat of revolution, or coerce them with laws. We should not have to beg or bribe them with tax reductions.

Chapter 5 - Stocks, Bonds and Speculation

What are goods and services worth? Demand to consume determines the value of our products, and demand creates a tenuous near-future value of resources and manufactured goods. We are so wrapped up in our incorrect understanding of money that we want to place money values on everything, instead of demand values. We buy and sell raw materials and resources without understanding that it is tomorrow's productive labor and future demand for goods that is necessary to allow us to barter and consume the materials being transformed and manufactured today.

Virtually everything we buy and sell, both wholesale and retail, is auctioned to the highest bidder daily; demand for goods and services are generally satisfied by competitive auction. The foundation of Capitalism is the auction process of exchanging property. The auction is the only manner in which private property and labor can be exchanged for the highest contemporary value. Every owner desiring to sell a product will make it available to all potential buyers and strike a deal with the highest bidder.

In a typical auction format an audience of potential buyers has an item presented and its virtues described, at which point those who desire to own the item respond to the auctioneer's offers to sell. The auctioneer calls out an asking price and if more than one person is willing to bid that price, a higher price is then asked until only one buyer is willing to pay the sum being asked. It is not the auctioneer who has raised the price of this item to its selling price. Prices increase with demand; therefore it is the bids of the would-be owners that establish a price. In the case of the single item at auction, the highest bidder has set the price. If an item is offered to a group of would-be consumers at one dollar, and one hundred people indicate they are willing to pay one dollar for the item, then there must be at least one hundred of that item available or the asking price will rise until the number of would-be consumers falls to match the available supply.

The auction format of buying and selling surrounds us. Even our daily purchases at the supermarket or department store are an auction. Buying or not buying different goods causes prices to fluctuate in response to our demands. When we want more of certain goods or services, the asking price is raised until the competition amongst those who want to consume does not increase above the available supply. And similarly if demand falls off, prices will have to fall or potential customers will continue to leave goods on the store shelves. Our willingness to consume or not consume throughout the year is our expression of our bids for goods and services.

Those who exchange the most surplus labor to acquire free raw materials in our economic system are then under a good deal of pressure to increase efficiency and productivity, in order to compete for market share and profits. Prices change hourly, daily, and monthly in our markets, depending on contractual arrangements, as well as current and projected consumption, therefore the value of our labor and resources changes as demand changes.

A stock market is an auction where representatives (called specialists) of stock brokerage companies meet to buy and sell stocks (corporate equity). Each brokerage firm that is a member of a stock exchange has employees that specialize in buying and selling stocks of certain industrial types. Each brokerage has enough specialists to be able to buy or sell any stock listed on their exchange. Brokerages also have employees and/or self-employed stockbrokers around the country who receive buy and sell orders from their customers, and relay those orders to their exchange broker who alerts the specialist that is responsible for the particular stock that is wanted, or offered for sale. The specialist then proceeds to the area of the exchange where that stock is traded and offers to buy or sell your stock, as the case may be, by dickering with specialists from other brokerages. The buying specialists group together, facing the selling specialists, prices to sell are announced and bids to purchase are made, with each side making some adjustments until trades are made. If you the customer have offered to buy or sell at the best market price available at that time, your order will be executed and you will receive a written record of that trade.

Like the stock market, commodities (food-stuffs and raw industrial materials) are traded in a similar manner. The value of all commodities varies with increasing and decreasing bids. There are no items whose value is unchangeable. If you want wheat or cotton or iron, you must first contact a commodity broker at some investment company who will act as your agent in procuring the raw materials you desire. The broker will do this by contacting an associate broker that buys and sells for his or her company in the auction pits of one of the commodity exchanges. When this floor broker is told what commodity you want to purchase and how much you are willing to pay, he or she will go to the area of the exchange where your resource is bought and sold and compete with other brokers to obtain that commodity for you at your bid price. If your bid is accepted, a bill of sale will be issued and arrangements for delivery can be made. If you need to acquire raw materials immediately to continue your business, you will most likely pay the current asking price. In any case, buyers and sellers are changing the prices that the buyer will pay or that the seller will accept minute by minute.

Similarly, if you wish to sell a commodity resource, you must contact a commodity broker and have him or her offer your goods at your asking price. If demand is strong and your price is reasonable to the market, your goods will be sold. If your asking price is high and you need to sell, your broker will need to lower the asking price bit by bit until a buyer is found. In contrast to the very slow auction of goods and services in retail stores, commodity auctions are extremely quick to change prices and very volatile in the size of price changes that can occur.

The bond market operates similarly in that a broker or investment banker must be used to buy or sell bonds. A great difference between commodities and stocks or bonds is that commodities are the real resources from which we manufacture all that we consume. Stocks represent ownership of manufacturing facilities, equipment, patents and distribution facilities. Corporate bonds represent loans to corporations to expand their productive capacity, with collateral for such bonds being manufacturing facilities, owned raw resources, equipment, etc. When you buy a bond you are acting as a bank, by loaning your money to the company issuing the bond; for which you are paid interest for the use of your money.

Originally stocks represented ownership of a company in the sense of equity, wherein the original sale of stock was insured by the collateral of manufacturing facilities and equipment, so that in the event a company went bankrupt, the stockholders would be somewhat compensated by the sale of buildings and equipment. Today, companies expand production or survive slow times by borrowing moneys from banks or through the sale of bonds, rather than creating and selling new stocks. They use company assets as collateral for those loans or bonds, which offers some protection to banks and bondholders and none to stockholders. If the company should fail, outstanding loans and bonds may be repaid out of the sale of equipment and property, if that equipment and property still have economic value.

If a company has assets of ten million dollars, and one million shares of stock are owned by the public, that stock is protected to a price of ten dollars per share. But if the value of that stock rises to one hundred dollars per share when speculators and investors bid up its price without regard to its equity value, then ninety-percent of that stock's value is unprotected by company assets and profits. Its price has been inflated in a careless and economically dangerous manner. If bonds are sold to raise ten million dollars for operating capital, then the company's assets will be used to guarantee those bonds and there will be no equity value in that stock. Bankruptcy for such a company would result in a total loss for stockholders.

For stockholders, their financial return as owners can be positive or negative. When a company makes a profit the stockholders can divide the profits amongst themselves. If a loss has occurred, they may need to contribute operating capital in exchange for bonds, sell bonds to new investors and thereby lose equity, or economize operations to eliminate losses. Stockholders also can receive a return on their stock by selling it to another would-be owner for more than they paid for it - a capital gain. If the company was doing poorly and a stockholder needed to sell his or her shares, they might have to sell for less than they paid - a capital loss.

Many corporations are more interested in how their stock price is viewed by speculators than by investors. When stock prices get somewhat above one hundred dollars per share, a round lot of one hundred shares would cost over ten thousand dollars. These higher prices tend to discourage speculators, who want to own lower price stocks, which are usually more volatile, allowing them to skim profits off that volatility; and high prices discourage small investors with limited capital, who cannot afford higher priced stocks. High stock prices therefore reduce the exchange activity of a stock (volatility); such that many corporations split their stock two-for-one or three-for-one, dropping the share price to one-half or one-third of its previous price, to encourage increased speculative buying of their stock.

Not all players in these markets are long-term investors, or consumers of resources and commodities; many are strictly short-term speculators, betting on price changes. Our economy is the production and consumption of goods and services made available by, and only by, the sum of all of our labors. To manipulate the economy outside of laborers bartering with other laborers, is to divert labor goods and services to run government, or to the idle rich, the idle poor, or to speculators and stock profiteers.

Speculators are people who bid to own, or offer to sell all sorts of stocks, bonds, and commodities, without holding stocks to receive dividends, or holding bonds to maturity, or taking possession of commodities to produce consumable products. Their gains come directly from other peoples' losses and their every effort is to try and read the markets, to be able to predict the actions of investors and consumers, and buy or sell on their own most favorable terms.

Speculation does not drive or strengthen the economy; it only feeds off the surplus of the economy. Speculators do not provide services and infrastructure. They have become institutionalized in our commercial real estate, bond, stock and commodity markets. Their actions in these markets conspire to create values for the pieces of paper that they buy and sell, which are different from the real market value of the assets represented by stocks, as well as the real market value of the commodities that speculators buy and sell, but never see. Political power is manipulated to regulate these investment markets for the benefit of speculators.

Speculation in stocks and other financial papers has caused the attention of the greedy to focus on the changing values of stocks, rather than on actual corporate earnings and dividends paid to investors. These changes in stock values are brought about more by the activity of speculators than by economic activities of production and consumption. The longevity of investment toward gain, from present and future profits of a company, is giving way to short term buying and selling, based solely on stock price. Speculation often drives many stock values way above or way below real current market values and earning capacity. These variations allow speculators to unduly influence trading in the markets, by encouraging investment for short-term gain through volatility, rather than long term gain via surplus labor gathered from the sales of goods and services. As the markets oscillate, speculators buy and sell to siphon off a portion of the flow of investment dollars coming at the markets. Whenever uncertainty arises, speculators (and investors turned into speculators by their brokers) drive the markets toward economic anarchy.

"The market is always right," investment brokers, referring to the value of stocks, bonds, and commodities often quote this statement to customers; hoping to impress them with a belief that the markets reflect overall attitudes of investors and speculators. But for every buyer of stocks and commodities there is a seller of the same. Therefore the markets are actually low as far as buyers are concerned and high as far as sellers are concerned. Neither group thinks the markets are right. The fact is, the markets are always changing. The direction of change is determined when there is a surplus of buyers over sellers (rising market) or vice versa. The market is only right when and if it stagnates with no change.

The greatest challenge to investors and speculators is the legal requirement that dealing in stocks and bonds must be a gamble. Forehand knowledge of information that will affect the value of a stock or bond is illegal, and is called insider trading. The government requires that all potential-players in the stock and commodity markets be equally informed of the present and equally ignorant of the future. Though there is great diversity of opinions about the meaning of corporate data, still all players must have equal access to that data.

It used to be that every stock trade was done face to face and that a particular stock would only be traded at one exchange. Today stocks are traded 24-hours a day; over the phone between customer and broker, via computer between brokerages, and on numerous stock exchanges around the world.

When stock trades were made face-to-face, trading was relatively slow even at its most volatile times. Now that brokerages can buy and sell stocks via computer, orders to buy and sell can be processed with lightning speed. Many speculators automatically offer their stocks for sale if the market should decline a certain amount, while others have standing orders to buy certain stocks if the market is rising. Standing orders to buy or sell at certain price levels tend to exaggerate the volatility of the market. They cause a rising market to rise further, or a declining market to fall further, than they would have without speculative standing orders.

Many investors buy stocks on margin (partial payment), paying only a portion of their cost. If the market drops far enough that their down-payment equals the loss on their stock, they then must immediately send more money to the brokerage firm that they bought it through. If investors do not respond to the margin call for additional money, their brokerage will sell their stock at any price, without their permission, and send them a bill if the brokerage had to pay the difference between their customers' down payment and the selling price. In such a case the investor has not only lost their stock or bonds and a chance to recoup their losses when that stock or bond regains market value, they may be saddled with additional debt to pay for losses beyond their control.

While your broker is trying to get you the best

deal available, you are actually competing with your broker's company to buy and sell stocks. Brokerages invest heavily in stocks, bonds and commodities, speculating for their own profit. So if you want to sell a stock that their chief strategists believe is going to go up, they will not necessarily inform you. More likely they will buy your stock from you and be quite happy to have you contribute to their welfare. Likewise, if you want to buy stock that they believe is going down, they will tell you so if they don't own any, or they will sell you theirs and remain happily silent. The real competition between you and your brokerage firm happens when you both want to buy or sell. In that case your brokerage will sell or buy a number of stock orders through the same specialist at the same relative time, and yours will be the ones with the least gains, making the ones with the most gains their trades. Brokerage firms look out for themselves at everyone's expense, including their customers.

While you are competing with your broker, consider what stock trades mean. There are thousands of stocks being traded, and some stocks may trade tens of thousands of times in one day while others do not trade at all. A stock can trade all day, going up and down and close at the same price as the previous day; or it could be higher all day and close lower because in the last trade of the day some selling specialist accepted a lower bid, and thereby sold some stock at a price below the previous day's closing price. That stock would have been reported as being down in price and value for that day's trading. How a stock performs throughout a trading session and how it performs at the end of a trading session may be two very different representations of the strength of that stock, but only the latter is reported.

Each stock transaction determines the value of all of the stock for a company. When one trade of 100 shares, usually the minimum amount which can be bought or sold, is made at a price above or below any current price, the value of all of a company's stock is considered to have risen or fallen by that same amount. And though many investors do not buy or sell on a daily basis, they still watch their stocks and note how their perceived net worth has increased or decreased as their stocks move up or down. The greatest of fallacies is the belief that one's stocks are worth the prices quoted daily in the paper. Only a small percentage of any company's stock needs to be placed on the market and sold at any price to wreak havoc in the value of all of that particular stock. A company's stock is worthless as soon as investors are unwilling to own all of it. By this I mean, if more of its stock is offered than the market can find buyers at any price, the value of all of that company's stock falls to zero, (no demand, no value).

For some companies the ups and downs of their stock is almost meaningless because they may own very little of their stock or they may not be using it for collateral to secure loans or bonds. While other companies may have borrowed heavily against the value of their stock, (owned by them) and if the value of that stock should fall below a certain level it could become insufficient collateral for outstanding loans. That company would be forced to buy them back at the original price from its cash flow, which would stifle its business or make it non-competitive. Or it may simply be forced into bankruptcy and have its assets sold to pay back the loans made against its fallen stock; leaving other holders of its stock to bear the loss of its value.

All stocks are in a false equilibrium day to day. Barring some catastrophe in the world in general, or some segment of our economy in particular, a stock's equilibrium is established by its previous day's activity. Each daily close of the markets establishes a new point from which gains or losses are measured. But since it is buyers and sellers who define this equilibrium, the ratio of buyers to sellers is very important to the value of a company's stock. In the mid-1950's the general investment in stocks was so limited and stock market activity was so sluggish that the market could not even absorb sales of General Motors stock at 20-thousand shares per day, without starting panic selling of that stock (and that is 20-thousand out of 350 million shares owned by the public at that time). Even today, with more investors and a much more volatile market that has much higher daily volumes of stock trades; only a very small percentage of any company's stock can be offered for sale on a daily basis to avoid a price plunge that would erase the equity value of that stock for all of its investors.

If there were an infinite number of buyers and sellers available to a market, it would be fairly stagnant and nearly impossible to crash. But there are only a finite number of buyers and sellers; both sides draw from the same pool of speculators and investors. Whenever the market falls, it is likely that many would-be buyers will become sellers, and many who were on the sidelines will step in to sell their stocks and avoid further losses. If sufficient pressure to sell stocks at any price occurs, even if only in one sector of the market, it can attract cash from other sectors, consume that capital and thereby reduce the cash available to support values in other markets. Pressure to sell for lower prices in one market can produce a downward momentum for all of the markets. As new prices are established at lower levels, equity is lost across the board, both for sellers and for owners who remain on the sideline hoping for stability. With any major loss of equity in one market, those needing to cover their losses may transfer or borrow capital from other areas of the economy to balance account sheets at brokerage firms. The loss of capital to investors in those other markets will cause prices to fall for them as well.

In 1987, many small investors could not get out of the stock market before being wiped out. This was not only a result of it being impossible to get through to your broker by phone, since many thousands of other investors were doing as you were. Your broker's company had two things to gain by your losses. It could sell its own stock first and consume what little demand may have existed to buy stocks, and it could keep your stock off the market to prevent prices falling even lower. When supply of anything exceeds demand, prices will fall relative to the available surplus and any demand to consume that surplus.

There is a method of selling stocks and commodities in our economy that is called selling-stock-short or short-selling. Short-selling is a way of creating a false surplus of a stock or commodity. In essence we borrow stock from some investor, through a broker, and we sell that stock to a third party because we believe that its price will fall in the future (we are selling short because we are short the amount of stock that we have borrowed and sold). At this point all we have done is sell something that does not belong to us, making neither a gain nor a loss. If our gamble is right and the price of that stock or commodity does fall, we can then buy that stock back from a fourth party at the lower price and return it to the person or brokerage we borrowed it from. Because we do not pay anything to borrow the stocks, our profit is the difference between the higher price we sold and the lower price we paid to have them returned to their original owner.

The history of selling-short is the most calamitous in all of our economic history. One hundred years ago professional stock traders were ruining each other and many sound businesses by selling large amounts of a particular stock short. Then they would put out rumors that caused other investors to also sell that stock, driving the price very low, which would allow them to make large profits by buying back that stock at a lower price and return it to the brokerage they had borrowed it from. Other traders who owned that stock on margin might go bankrupt, unable to cover a sudden and unexpected loss due to unfounded rumors. The company that issued that stock may have other shares held as collateral for expansion loans. If the price of the stock should fall, the loss of price equity would force banks to call for other collateral, or they might seize property, take over a company's management and possibly liquidate it. If a company had cash assets that would allow it to buy up these short sales as they occurred, it would not only support the price of their stock, but as less and less stock was available for investors to own, the price of a company's stock could rise. The short-sellers would eventually have to buy stocks to replace those that they had sold short. This would create demand for a reduced supply, causing the price to rise and possibly catastrophic losses for those who had sold short. The Japanese do not allow selling-short in their markets, and for good reason. There have been many stock panics in our history and all of them have been worsened by selling-short.

Consider a long time investor-A, who owns stock outright and is as much concerned with dividends as stock prices. If this stock is managed by a brokerage for that investor-A; the brokerage could loan that stock to speculator-B, who would sell it on the market to speculator-C. If investor-A did not want to sell, there would be less stock available to the market and the price would remain higher; forcing speculator-C to offer a higher price to entice an investor to sell some stock. But since speculator-B is borrowing and then selling this stock, he is helping his own gamble by adding this borrowed stock for sale to the market, thereby encouraging a price decrease simply by increasing supply. If the price does fall, speculator-B has made a profit when he buys stock from investor-D (who could actually be investor-A dumping the stock to avoid further loss) and returns it to the brokerage. In essence the brokerage has aided and abetted a loss to one of its investor customers, while helping a speculator customer profit. Selling-short does not increase investor equity; however, it does reduce it by the amount of profit made by the short-seller.

So why do stockbrokers offer short selling? Simply to make money; stockbrokers earn a fee each time stock is traded. They do not like investors who purchase stocks and then hold them for years to earn dividends. They want the fees associated with trades and market volatility, and they are happy to help speculators hurt investors. If they can they will turn all investors into speculators.

There is a big difference between investors and speculators. Investors put surplus money in the stock, bond and commodity markets for the long term. They hold stocks for years to receive dividends as a return on capital investment. They buy bonds and hold them to maturity and receive interest payments. They buy commodities and use them to manufacture goods and provide foodstuffs. While the speculator is a pure gambler, buying and selling stocks, bonds and commodity contracts based on price changes, seldom holding them to receive dividends or interest. Only a speculator would sell a stock or commodity short. Only a speculator would buy or sell a stock index contract, betting that the market as a whole will go up or down. Only a speculator would take an option to buy stocks, or sell stocks, rather than commit fully.

As more money flows through the markets to

speculate in price changes rather than dividend or interest returns, the volatility of price changes will increase. When earnings reports are low or below market expectations, many stocks fall in price rapidly and somewhat drastically as speculators dump those stocks knowing that with bad reports other speculators will sell such stocks and others will temporarily choose not to buy. In a non-speculative market a stock would drift lower in price, or stagnate for some time. So speculators will move out early, and even sell the markets short to accelerate a decline brought on by perceived weakness, and reap profits for themselves thereby.

Not everyone in the markets is a speculator. If this were the case we would have daily panics and weekly chaos. But the amount of activity in the markets that is strictly speculation is increasing, and we can see this in the changing relationship between dividends and prices. How can a stock, which returns a 4% quarterly dividend to a market that was expecting 5%, have its price drop 5% or more in one day? In the opposite case, the stock price might rise 5% in one day on a dividend of only 1% above market expectations. Investors would not sell or buy enough stock on this information alone to make any noticeable price changes. Only speculators can do this, because speculators are working a pure gamble, based on near term strength or weakness of companies.

If you find it hard to compare the gambling in Las Vegas with the gambling on the New York Stock Exchange, consider the activities of each. In Las Vegas you enter a gambling casino, exchange dollars for tokens or chips and proceed to wager that certain events will occur according to your predictions. When you put money on a number at Roulette you are predicting (or at the very least hoping) that the marble will stop on your number. When you place bets in a card game you are predicting that your cards count higher than others' cards, in your game. When you put coin or tokens in a Slot machine you are predicting that the machine's parts will randomly align themselves in such a way that more money will be returned to you than you will put into the machine. All of these activities are called gambling because you are spending and receiving items of value, money; and because you may only do so legally if you cannot accurately predict the outcome of your wagers. For every winner there is a loser, if the house is the winner then the customer is the loser, and vice versa.

If you choose to place wagers on the New York Stock Exchange, you must also place money at risk and presumably be as ignorant, or at least as deluded, as other players. First you hire a broker and put money into an account, from which your broker can deduct funds when you wish to buy stocks, and into which your brokerage can put your winnings, should you be so lucky. You may contact your broker and tell him or her which stocks you would like to buy, and how much to pay. You now own a piece of some company, and your voice counts in managing your corporation, according to the percentage of ownership in your name. Your bet is that your workers and management team are going to out-produce the competition, make greater profits and return a larger dividend to you. If your corporation does do better you not only win with dividends, but your shares of stock are likely worth more than you paid. Other potential players will see the stronger position of your corporation and some of them will bid more money to buy into your game. If you should decide to sell your stock allowing someone else to take your place and risk, you will receive more money than you paid. This profit is called a capital gain.

If you guessed wrong and your corporation operated inefficiently and lost money, you would not get a dividend, and your stock might drop drastically in value, because more owners may want to sell than there are would-be owners waiting to buy. Sellers are forced to accept less and less for their stocks, potentially resulting in great losses for some. For every one who wins someone else has lost. The big difference in these two gambling industries is the length of time between wagers and the determination of profit or loss.

Brokerages that facilitate stock, bond and commodity trading, operate in a similar manner and purpose to companies that operate gambling casinos. Brokerages do not care if the markets go up or down, so long as trades are being made. The brokerages charge a fee for each trade; the more trades, the more income for brokerages. In gambling casinos the odds of winning slightly favor the casino owners when one bets against the casino; and the casinos charge players a fee for the use of their facilities when players gamble with each other. The casino owners' interest also lies in the volume of gambling; the greater the activity, the greater the income for the casinos.

Besides brokerage firms operating as very large players in these markets, there are also thousands of mutual fund companies speculating in all of the investment markets. If you buy into a stock mutual fund, you are pooling your dollars with many other investors and paying a professional stock trader to buy and sell for you. Your holdings in such a company is not in individual stocks, but as a percentage of the value of all of that fund's holdings, calculated by comparing your investment with the total of all dollars contributed by all members of your fund. These mutual funds have become very big players in these markets. Mutual fund managers make their wages and bonuses by having the value of their stock and bond holdings rise in price value over what was initially paid.

Brokerage firms reap their wages and bonuses through fees from the number of stock, bond, or commodity transactions occurring. If the markets are sluggish, with relatively little trading going on, brokerages can buy and sell stocks and bonds with other brokers, kiting stock, bond and commodity values and thereby creating a mirage of investment activity. This practice is very old and is called, "Churning the market". This is principally done to provide them with cash flow and protect their stock, bond and commodity portfolios, since their net worth (and the value of their own stock) is tied to cash on hand and market value of their investments. This churning hurts on-going investment activity, because it prevents the markets from moving lower and allowing investors an opportunity to purchase stocks, bonds and commodities at a true market value.

In the United States there are three principal markets to buy and sell stock. The New York exchanges are the primary market, and the over the counter exchanges are the secondary market (NASDAQ). There is another exchange market for stocks and bonds that is referred to, as the "Third Market". The third market is a partial joining of these two markets to facilitate the selling of large blocks of stock. Which if they were offered through an exchange to individual investors would crash that stock's value, along with its paper equity, and could create large declines in the overall market if not panic and chaos.

The third market is composed of brokerages that will buy large offerings individually, or in concert with other buyers, at a set price and then resell it in small lots in the usual manner. Though the set price for these large sales is determined by prices set at auction in the exchanges, this stock is not being auctioned. It is being sold in a manner contrary to the rules of the exchanges, that all stock sales be offered in public via an auction to let buyers and sellers determine market price and value. The seller of a large block of stock is guaranteed through the third market to receive the highest possible price for such stocks or bonds, at the expense of unwary buyers in the regular auction markets. One person's loss is another person's gain in these markets. In the public exchange markets, if a large block of stock is offered at a price no buyer is willing to pay, it will then remain unsold or only a portion of it will sell. If it must be sold, then the price must drop until buyers agree that it has dropped to its proper value, according to supply and demand in a free market. The third market is just a creation of a controlled market to allow brokerage firms to protect the value of their own holdings and to prevent investors from profiting when other market-players' must sell.

The exchanges could have barred the sale of large blocks of stock, or limited the size and timing of all sales, but this would obviously not be a free market with prices determined by supply and demand. So they maintain the illusion of a free market by withholding knowledge and access to participate in sales, such as the third market, from the public. If the third market were a small market, as compared to the exchanges, little harm would be done to investors. But the third market is not small, it is very large and very controlled to maintain higher prices, requiring individual investors to pay more than a free market would require for many stocks and bonds.

Consider a stock market very different from the market that has developed; a new market, where brokers facilitate buying and selling but own no stock themselves. A market where short selling is illegal, and where speculation is suppressed by not permitting a purchased stock to be resold in less than 30 days without a significant penalty tax paid to the federal government. Similarly for bonds, the sale of a bond would be final, until redeemed at maturity, or a penalty greater than its lifetime yield would be assessed. And in the commodity markets only those who produce commodities could sell contracts up to the amount they can produce, and only those companies that process and consume those commodities could buy contracts, up to the amount they have a track record of consuming.

Markets with these restrictions would require different corporate structures. Workers and communities would be the largest and most stable investors in the companies they worked for or the communities they are located in. The raising of capital and investment in production would follow the path of vested interest. Which would require most corporations to be publicly owned and operated, for the benefit of consumption without debt.

Market investments like stocks, bonds and commodities are considered to be barometers, gauging the health of our economy. Market watchers are always trying to forecast future economic activity based on current activity and market trends. Trends and market activity, however, are no better barometers to predict the future than reading tealeaves. Economic activity is much more a barometer of what the markets should do than the other way around. This money circulating in these markets has no direct bearing on general economic activity associated with the production and consumption of goods and services.

Because most stock trades are between one investor and another or one speculator and another, wherein the company that issued the stock is in no way involved, the stock market could go out of business without having a catastrophic economic impact on society in general. Certainly all of the people employed in operating the stock market would be devastated, and the general misunderstanding of how these markets operate would cause psychological panic amongst other industries and the public in general, which could lead to a complete economic collapse. But such a collapse would be as unnecessary as having our whole economy collapse if Los Vegas were put out of business by a major earthquake. Certainly the workers and owners of all of the casinos and related businesses would be financially distressed and have to seek other opportunities. But the rest of society would not need to go into a panic. We deal with catastrophic weather and geological events affecting our lives and economy every year, and we take them in stride. Problems in gambling industries should never be perceived as causing negative economic impacts. A panic in the stock market could only spread to our productive economy if people are ignorant of what the stock market represents and how it operates; but then if people knew how these markets functioned they probably would avoid them altogether.

      The stock market is very much a balloon market, because it contains so much air (presumed equity). For example, consider a small stock market with just ten companies. Each company has sold 10,000 shares to the public, and each company's stock is currently listed at $10.00 per share. Since stocks usually sell in lots of one hundred shares, each lot is worth $1,000.00. Each company's total shares are worth $100,000.00; making the total value of all ten companies stocks to be $1,000,000.00. If one trader comes into this market and offers $11.00 per share to purchase one hundred shares of Company-A stock, then he or she has paid a total of $1,100.00, but has only increased the real equity of that one lot of one hundred shares by $100.00. The market, however, reports that all 10,000 shares of that company's stock are up and valued at $11.00 per share. One hundred dollars has created $10,000.00 in presumed equity, for this one company's ten thousand shares of stock. All of that increased value is a fraud, because the original $100.00 in additional value went to the seller, and is in no way further associated with Stock-A. Now consider that if the seller of stock in Company-A takes the $1,100.00 and invests it in one hundred shares of Company-B, another $10,000.00 in air is created. Continue this from B to C, C to D, etc.

until the seller of Company-J's stock winds up with the $1,100.00 and is out of the market. All ten companies' stock has gone up ten percent and the $100.00 in additional equity has exited the market. One hundred dollars has created $100,000.00 in paper equity in just ten trades and is out of this market, as is all money invested in stocks, it is always outside the market, the seller has the money, but no stock. Obviously, the real stock markets are much larger, with millions upon millions of stock trades daily. This unreal and presumed equity can certainly be taken out of the market in a similar manner, since so much of what is reported as equity gains is only air.

All stock purchases are transacted by bringing money from outside the market to trade with those who own stocks and would be willing to leave the market, becoming non-owners, if they are paid their price. The sellers exit the market, even if only temporarily, with the money that was never in the market. Trading your current surplus labor for stocks will only net you a gain if in the future someone else is willing to trade you more surplus labor for the right to own your stocks. Your money is not in the stock, bond, or commodity markets; it is in the pocket of the person that sold you stocks, bonds, or commodities. Both today and in the future, the un-inflated value of stocks is the fire-sale value of equity in buildings and equipment and resources that are not collateral for loans and bonds. Everything else is a mirage, appearing as inflated equity created by too much surplus labor being exchanged (gambled) for control of corporations and their future profits. This "air" in the market is why price changes can be so volatile; small changes up or down on small amounts of a company's stock are leveraged to affect all of its stock by and because of investor ignorance.

Let me digress a moment to another discussion of money, in the realm of buying and selling as done in the stock market. All money available to purchase any asset is pocket money, in the context of liquidity. It is not invested in stocks and bonds, or real estate, or gems and precious metals, or stamps and rare coins. Money simply moves from one pocket to another (from one bank account to another), in trade for assets or consumption of goods. Those who purchase stocks and bonds, or real estate, etc., take money out of their pockets to effect a purchase, while those who sell stocks and bonds, or real estate, etc., put money into their pockets to affect a sale of those goods. The key to the future value of any commodity, or stock, or piece of land bears directly on the amount (and trade value) of pocket money available at any given future time. These markets are devoid of any value other than future demand to own stocks, bonds, commodities and real estate; and that demand will depend on the mount of pocket money available for investment or speculation. The money is always outside the markets because it only moves from one pocket to another, wherein the last pocket always belongs to someone who is NOT IN THE MARKET.

While investment in the stock market is considered to be a capital investment in our productive economy, it very seldom is. If you are able to purchase new stock directly from a corporation that will use that money to expand their productive capacity, then you are investing capital in our economy. But when a stock is sold the second, third and so on... times, the new owner is not investing in that corporation. The vast majority of stock trades are done between one investor-speculator and another, trading places between would-be owners and those who would rather not be owners. As far as our productive economy is concerned, these dollars serve no useful purpose. They create no jobs, build no factories, nor do they feed or shelter anyone, except stockbrokers and speculators. The taxes paid on gains are offset by the deductions taken on losses. Brokers and the people that keep these markets going are all on capital welfare. They facilitate these gamblers in transferring money and stocks, and charge a fee to do so. But unless they are helping a corporation issue new stock, they are just recording the economically irrelevant bets of their customers. Stockbrokers and Bookmakers (that manage bets on horses, or sporting events, or whatever) are that same animal in twin professions.

Many baby-boomers are being encouraged to invest in personal savings accounts like IRA's to benefit their uncertain retirement. And many of these IRA's are invested in the stock market, bringing additional dollars to the New York style gambling industry. This money is simply inflating stock prices and giving the illusion of equity growth. Remember, money put into an IRA or 401K, to buy stocks and bonds, is going into the pockets of the sellers. To reap your reward as a seller when you need retirement money, you are betting there will be more buyers in the future willing to pay more to own your stocks and bonds than was the case when you purchased. Such reasoning is how pyramid schemes operate. The boomers are buying into a pyramid scheme that is shrinking at its base (without exception, all pyramid schemes fail); the following generation will be too small in population and earning capacity to bid up prices and produce a profit for the boomers to retire on. The generations following the Boomers are going to have their income taxed heavily to pay the Social Security and Medicare for the Boomers and thereby will not have the pocket money to buy into IRA's and 401K's; causing those markets to fall catastrophically in value and bankrupt many Boomers. Consider also that most 401K plans are not invested in industrial stocks and bonds; rather they are only speculating on the profitability of a mutual fund company, i.e., the stock you own and will need to sell at a higher price to have retirement income is your investment firm's stock, and no other. Since your fund managers must buy and sell stocks and bonds, etc. to make a profit, similar to all other mutual funds, you can only come out a winner if other 401K speculators come out losers. The Boomers will either suffer losses that will destroy the value of their retirement investments, or they may be forced to keep their capital tied up in owning stocks and bonds and only receive relatively small dividends, without ever being able to recover and spend their invested capital.

The game of win or lose goes like this. If investor-A buys some stock costing one hundred dollars per share and it rises in value to one hundred ten dollars per share, at which time investor-A sells to investor-B; investor-A has made ten dollars per share profit. If this stock continues to rise to one hundred twenty dollars per share and investor-B sells to investor-C, then investor-B has also made ten dollars per share profit. If this stock falls back to one hundred dollars per share and investor-C sells this stock, then investor-C has suffered a loss exactly equal to the previous gains. Similarly, if this stock had dropped for investor-A & -B but rises for investor-C, the initial losses would equal the final gain. For every gain their will ultimately be an equivalent loss, and for every loss their will be an equivalent gain, the books are always balanced. Brokerage fees, taxes and inflation operate to guarantee that in the long run, less money leaves these markets as investor profits than comes into them as gambling wagers. Over time those who profit from these markets do so only by losses incurred by others. Periodic panics and crashes in these markets balance the books by creating the losses that equal the year over year gains for the years between such panics and crashes.

Many investment counselors tout the fact that prices for stocks have risen faster than general inflation for over sixty years. This is only true on average; yet it took forty years (until 1969) for the stock market to have prices surpass stock prices of the summer of 1929, in dollar amounts that were still significantly less in dollar value because of inflation. For that 40-year period investors only made money through dividends. But price increases are inflation, such that there has been more inflation of stock prices in the past seventy years than general inflation, especially in the last few years. Those who bought stocks many years ago are now enjoying large capital gains, over and above general inflation. But today's purchaser of stocks is paying much more for stocks, as compared to other goods, than in the past. The capital gains of yesterday's long-term investors may become the capital losses for today's short-term speculators, since for every gain in these markets there will eventually be a loss.

The featuring by the news media, over the years, of catastrophic losses by certain international banks, or certain brokerage firms, or individual investors, shows the general ignorance of how these gambles work. If we heard news of a poker game wherein three players lost $50,000 each, but a fourth player won $150,000, we would not dwell on the losers and the tragic consequences of their losses, without mentioning the winner. More likely, we would focus on the winner and attempt to associate ourselves with such winners, and generally ignore the losers. In the financial markets losses may be tragic to one person or corporation, but on the principle that gains equal losses, both are irrelevant to the market and to the economy. If governments, market directors or investor-speculators alter their market strategies based on someone's losses, they are forgetting someone else's gains, implying that they do not understand these markets and ought not to be in them. Reporting gains and losses in any of the markets is a camouflage of fraud to keep unwary investors in the game. These markets are a zero net sum, so gains and losses are irrelevant. But since these con-games require continuous inflow of surplus productive labor to support brokers and investment bankers, there is an industry of reporting and describing activity in these markets that operates on a foundation of collusion of ignorance and obfuscation of facts.

Our government is a player in these markets, through the investment and banking regulations written into law, or the lack of prudent regulation in the face of greed. Consider the savings and loan fiasco of the 1980's, when real estate speculators and bankers financed real estate investment pyramids with junk bonds. These promises on paper were sold to unwary customers of the savings and loan banks, enticing them to take their savings, that were regulated and insured by the government, and invest them in bonds paying higher interest rates. Much of the money raised by selling these bonds was not regulated by government as to how it could be used. It was then loaned to speculators to purchase and develop real estate, far beyond the needs of our economy. Speculation in real estate kited prices above justifiable values, and could only be maintained by a pyramid of new investments (pyramids always self-destruct). When it became apparent to the speculators that many of their properties were very much over valued, they simply dumped them on the savings and loans, which held the mortgages on the real estate, or held investment portfolios full of junk bonds, which were bought to finance speculators' kiting schemes. When the savings and loan banks foreclosed on over-priced and over-developed properties, they had to sell them at auction, often at a great loss to their banks. Which meant that those fore-closed properties would not generate any income to pay the bondholders, thus the banks and developers could not pay back the junk bonds that had paid for the development of those properties, and which were _uninsured_ by federal deposit insurance. Many savings banks defaulted on their bond obligations and were closed by the government. With their - insured depositors turned into uninsured investors - being the big losers in the whole scheme. Speculators put as little of their own money at risk as possible, preferring to borrow the surplus labor money of the middle class, in the form of high interest junk bonds issued through banks and other investment institutions. They know that the government can arrange for middle class taxpayers to bail out middle class depositors, when upper class speculators take the money and run.

Ultimately it will be the consumer who is the final winner or loser when they exchange their labor for the labor-goods in the marketplace. The system is closed, so that outside of natural disasters and war, every loss is associated with a gain. Speculators gained and taxpayers lost, when the 500 billion dollar savings and loan bailout was foisted on the working class.

Our government, under Ronald Reagan, took pride in deregulating the savings and loan industry. Where savings were invested in house and apartment construction and all transactions were insured, regulated and often guaranteed by our government. A very important and chief function of government is to regulate. To abandon regulation is to abandon government. After the anarchy allowed by de-regulation in the savings and loan scandal, the government then reasserted its obligation to regulate, and takes pride in burying the taxpayers 500 billion dollars deeper in debt.

Another act of government that precipitated economic problems were the tax reductions of the eighties, which benefited the wealthy most; who then directed more surplus money into the speculation markets. Speculation in commercial real estate became a pyramid until the economy stalled; leaving some community banks and savings and loans banks with many foreclosed properties that paid them no income. Income they needed to pay depositors interest on savings deposits. Many community banks needed to lower the interest rates offered to depositors to remain profitable and retain community savings in their banks, but competition forced them to pay more than many of them could afford. They were forced to compete with the federal government's offers of high interest yields, paid for investment in government bonds through money market banks. The government needed to borrow from those same depositors, after it lowered taxes a few years earlier, causing its income to become insufficient to support itself. Where everyone could have won, everyone has lost. A canyon of government debt is destroying the road that lies before us.

There is another force in the markets that is nearly invisible and that may be as much a threat to many investors as speculation. That threat is technology. Technology is changing so rapidly that it is now constantly devaluing equipment and patent equity. New ways of doing things are changing whole industries and making old equipment or methods obsolete in such a short time, that there is no transition time for competitors to adjust and maintain their customer base. So companies that only appear to be threatened have speculators and investors running away. These sorts of technology changes promote speculation over investment and put pressure on investors to become price speculators. Companies that look solid today may not exist long enough to payoff bonds or worker pensions.

When the stock market rises in value on a fixed number of companies and shares of stock in circulation, it can only represent either or both of the following economic conditions. Either inflation is taking place in the overall economy and can show up in higher bids for the available stocks; or an inflation of just stocks and bonds can take place when surplus labor is transferred from consumption of goods and services to investment and speculation.

Technology has allowed us to increase our surplus labor, and has allowed the owners of that surplus labor to invest it in many ways. Those who would use their surplus to acquire ownership of the limited resources and factories end up competing with each other, offering more and more money to buy out the current owners. This is the classic relationship of two many dollars chasing too few goods, prices rise to consume the surplus, and the result is inflation. Inflation like this happens in real estate, new technology, medical care, etc., from time to time. And from the net effect of these different types of inflation, the general inflation of our whole economy should be calculated.

However, if ever-increasing gains must be made so that resources will constantly be available to facilitate our existence, then ever increasing amounts of surplus labor must be taken from the laborers to pay for it. More people in the system can mean more production and more consumption, but not more ownership. As the pressure to consume increases, the system tends toward fewer owners, because they will gain through consumption demand, greater amounts of surplus labor from the workers to buy and consolidate their resource wealth; from which they can disparage society by controlling the flow of their resources into our economies. So our economy goes up and down, up and down, up and down.

The money traded for stocks is not capital in the sense of our collective productivity and potential productivity. It may be the capital of each investor, but when it rolls around in the stock market it is not available as capital to expand the economy. Investment in stocks is actually removing capital from our production-consumption economy. As more personal capital is brought to the gambling casino of the stock markets, less capital is available for producers to increase productivity. Stock brokers love bull markets because the increased buying and selling means more commissions are being paid to the brokerage firms. A bull market is a drag on economic expansion, not a boost; it attracts surplus labor away from the banks that make the loans that can facilitate business expansion and new job opportunities, to pay the wages and profits of the stock, bond, and commodity brokers. This is just another form of social welfare for the non-productive labor of stock, bond, and commodity brokers and investment bankers.

Chapter 6 - Inflation

It is somewhat of a strange thought to consider the value of money as always changing. We prefer to think that money-value is as solid as a rock, and goes on forever. We want money to be a real thing unto itself, because we believe that it is the source of wealth, and security from want. But money changes in value according to the amount of it available to exchange with the amount of goods and services available for consumption; supply and demand as it were.

In an expanding economy there is usually more demand for goods and services than current production can satisfy, so prices rise to control demand and to supply capital to expand production. As long as additional labor is available to hire, this inflation is rather mild. If labor supply is short and demand for additional labor is strong, wages could rise and bring about higher prices to pay higher wages; all this could lead to a spiraling period of inflation between wages and prices.

While in a deflating economy, more goods are available than there is demand (or ability) to consume. Competition amongst manufacturers will result in lower prices, lower profits, layoff of workers, and reduction of production. So prices fall (deflation), wages fall, and production and employment fall to match the decreasing demands of the economy. There is of course the danger that reductions in employment will lead to further reductions in demand, spiraling into a depression.

Inflation and deflation are always with us; they are a reflection of how we are dealing with each other. We say that demand is reduced when the economy falters and consumers reduce spending. Actually demand for goods and services are always expanding. What is being reduced is the amount of productive labor dollars available for laborers to barter with other laborers. This causes an undesirable reduction in consumption and production, but not demand.

The labor-value of our dollars in circulation is determined by dividing them by the productive labor on-going at that time. For example, if we have ten million dollars in circulation to purchase each one million hours of productive labor; then labor has an average dollar value of ten dollars per hour. And profit and taxes being ignored, the spending of ten dollars should purchase goods representing one hour of productive labor. If the amount of dollars doubles to twenty million in circulation for each one million hours of productive labor then wages will increase to twenty dollars per hour on average, and the cost to purchase goods and services will increase to twenty dollars per hour of productive labor. Similarly, if the number of dollars remains constant, but productive labor decreases by half, there are still twice as many dollars in relation to productive labor. So the value of the remaining productive labor will become twenty dollars per hour and the cost to purchase an hour of productive labor in the form of goods and services will be twenty dollars. For those who are working, these changes in the amount of dollars to productive labor represent a constant lag in obtaining fair value and fair prices for their labor when they spend their labor dollars.

An increased money supply is almost always associated with trade imbalances, where a country's surplus goods are either not competitive overseas, or are insufficient to balance imports. The importing nation pays its trade debts with newly issued money, rather than from the sale of its own goods and services. The exporting countries will bring that money back to the importing nation to purchase its goods and services or land and resources (temporary balanced trade). Domestic prices will rise to consume this new money and the value of domestic goods and services will become inflated; the same will happen with land and resources in nations that allow trade deficits.

On the other hand, if our Federal Reserve does not create new dollars to pay trade debts, those dollars will eventually come out of our domestic economy when importers use our domestic money supply to pay the foreign manufacturers, until there are not enough dollars left to maintain our domestic economy. Economic activity will decline, unemployment will rise and recession will occur until our national productivity is in balance with national consumption and the dollars available. Economic activity would continue to decline until we cannot afford to continue buying foreign goods, forcing us to accept foreign-held U.S. dollars back into our economy. The return of dollars will cause inflation in our natural resources and real estate, as those dollars disperse and circulate in an economic environment of reduced productivity. Trade imbalances can only portend inflation and loss of control of our natural resources, which will result in a reduced standard of living for the average citizen.

Two more chronic types of inflation are brought about by increased population and reduced resources. If the Earth had unlimited resources; if technology were simple and limited; an expanding population would be beneficial in that more people would mean more surplus labor. More surplus labor would provide more goods and services to the world economy, or it would allow people to labor less and still receive sufficient goods and services. But the Earth does not have unlimited resources. Energy, clean water, arable land, fish, and timber, are examples of resources that are being depleted, and which require more and more production labor to barter for consumption privileges. Since the totality of our labor produces and consumes the totality of resources made available to our economy, we can expect that as the population increases and resources decrease, the amount of labor that the owners of the resources can demand for their limited goods, will always increase to consume the labor available. The result is unavoidable inflation of labor-cost for everyone as the population grows, which will equate with reduced consumption for the same or higher cost.

More for some means less for others. Less food, less land, less education, less access to resources, less political representation, less access to medical care, less access to legal services, less opportunity overall. When you labor more today than you did in the past, to receive the same or reduced goods and services, you are experiencing cost inflation.

For years we have paid our trade debts with new dollars that have remained overseas to be used by many foreign economies. Many under-developed countries, and even black market economies, use U.S. dollars to trade for goods and services in place of their own inflating currencies. When the dollar is no longer useful as an international currency, our foreign dollars will come back to the U.S. and we will be forced to provide goods and services or properties and resources for foreigners to consume, in exchange for those repatriated dollars. When those returning dollars compete with our domestic dollars for the limited resources in the U.S., our prices will go up drastically until the costs for goods and services and resources equals the amount of money that will be competing to own them. Countries like France have often remarked that it is unfair that the U.S. can pay its foreign debts in its own currency, which no other country can do. But they should not be envious of this practice. When we pay our trade debt with new dollars we are simply sending overseas the guarantee of our own future inflation and economic destruction.

Probably the greatest source of inflation is war. War requires a great deal of resources to undertake. The amount of labor necessary to engage in war, and the power of those who command to take whatever goods and services available to conduct a war, will create shortages that will cause prices to soar. Many products may not be available at any price. War also destroys stored labor, buildings and homes, highways and railroads, dams and power plants; along with the loss of human life and the surplus labor that it represents. War reduces everyone's standard of living, requiring survivors to labor more and receive less. This, again, is cost inflation.

If goods are made less durable, then we suffer the cost inflation of having to replace more often the things that establish our standard of living. This consumes more of our labor, and unless we receive wage increases to offset shoddy products, our standard of living is reduced. This principle can certainly run in reverse, providing added value to our wage labor when the goods we purchase serve us longer than we had expected. However, it is not the nature of greed to give product durability away.

Other factors affecting industrial inflation are productivity and competition. Competition often forces higher productivity, which allows for lower selling prices, until the less efficient manufacturers are forced to abandon that market to those who can make a profit.

When I was growing up, in the 50's and 60's, we were led to believe that industry, through technology, would make virtually everything stronger, longer lasting, even indestructible. But planned obsolescence was instituted to keep some factories going. And widely manufactured goods created very competitive markets, wherein low profits forced many companies to make their products more and more cheaply, which not only served future sales through planned obsolescence, but also forced their competition to do likewise. Consumers are generally forced by need and naiveté to pay as little as possible for goods and services, preferring low initial cost, even with repeated replacement, in place of long term durability.

Another way inflation enters an economy is through changes in the amount of their labor a person is allowed to keep, to exchange in the marketplace. Government, on all levels, extracts a portion of our labor as taxes, to provide certain services and infrastructure by which we maintain and expand our economy and care for the indigent. Government may have to take more of our labor, for any number of reasons, presumably for our collective benefit, leaving us less labor to barter for the same goods we enjoyed previously. We will have to labor more hours to maintain our usual standard of consumption, or do without. Reduced purchasing power is identical with increased prices as far as consumption is concerned. Inflation of labor input also occurs when we must continue working forty hours per week to maintain our standard of living even though technology has increased to allow us to greatly reduce the labor input needed to make our goods. Working forty hours per week to produce twice the goods produced a generation ago, but only having the same relative standard of living, means that one-half of your labor is taken by owners for their benefit or by government through taxes to give to non-producers.

We also have evolved a somewhat complex system of manufacturing, transporting, and merchandising the products of our labor. We have several levels of cost and profit controlling the supply of goods and services from raw resources to the retail market. We have increased costs to buy products based on demand, even when costs to produce have not gone up. We may purposely decrease supply, causing prices to rise, to take advantage of persistent demand, causing consumers to have to offer more of their labor today to consume the same goods and services they enjoyed yesterday. This is simply a diverting of more productivity (cost inflation) from consumers to manufacturers and retailers.

Inflation can also come into an economy through cheaper labor. We are all familiar with large corporations closing plants here, and moving outside the country where cheaper labor is available. This causes former employees to seek other work, often for lower wages, which lowers their standard of living. When one's wages are reduced it has the same effect as raising the labor costs on the goods and services that one must consume. Likewise, additional workers enter the work force and compete for the available jobs, causing wages to lag behind general goods and services costs. Again, this is inflation of costs brought about by the decline in wage value. Labor is labor, and one hour's productivity in menial tasks cannot be discounted against another person's more technical or white-collar tasks.

Finally, we have the inflation of machine productivity. As we continually turn to technology to do more, faster; we wrongly believe that our standard of living is raised, free of any economic penalties. The owners of the resources may benefit from increased productivity and a competitive edge in the marketplace, but the workers displaced by machines are forced to find other work, often for a lower wage that translates into cost inflation for those laborers. Reduced labor per item produced in a factory does not necessarily translate into greater labor wages expended in the community. If the community were the employer, then labor saving machines would translate into greater freedom for workers to pursue other types of productive labor, thereby enriching the community. However, in private enterprise the owners of production gain increased profits from technology, which are not properly taxed. They are allowed to pare away their unneeded workers, often forcing the laborers of the whole community to carry the burden of those long unemployed. The employed laborer carries the unemployed, not the stockholders.

In our modern world we use the label Capitalism to describe the manner in which businesses develop, operate and compete for profit. Capitalism is not new; as long as people have produced surpluses of goods, they have used part of their surplus to support new productions or explorations that would increase the invested surpluses.

Capitalism has been the driving social force of Europe, Asia and Africa for thousands of year. Every empire, even the domination of a few villages by a stronger village, did so through the economy of Capitalism founded on surpluses. Empires and economies built on slavery are pure Capitalism, because slavery and indenture, even self-indenture for a set wage, is the foundation of producing surpluses for a benefit of a few over the wants and needs of the many. People have been forced, since the beginning of history, to perform labor and produce surpluses to be controlled by others.

The production and control of surpluses has led to another capitalistic principle that is continually operating to dominate social economies; that principle is INTEREST on debt (USURY); the loaning of surpluses to others and receiving more future surplus in return, as the payment (profit) on the use of today's surplus.

The vast majority of people today have been raised under economic conditions where interest earnings on savings and investments are honorable as well as profitable. But interest profits are ultimately destructive to Capitalism and to stable economies.

Interest income is a profit on unneeded surpluses, creating even larger surpluses for their owners; which are then recycled as loans to businesses and consumers to gather even greater future surpluses. These cycles would tend to domination and control of economies if they were not to a certain degree self-destroying.

If a given economy produces a surplus of goods and services over and above the demands of that economy, that surplus will be a waste of labor and resources. If, however, the payment for productive labor (wages) can be kept below its true labor exchange value, businesses can produce goods to meet demands by extending credit (loans) to consumers of their products. Such loans create additional profits for business that will be used to expand production or support more loans for more consumption. The consumer pays a higher price as well as interest on such loans to a point where most of their labor is spent servicing consumption loans that put them in debt for many years to come.

The whole debt edifice that grows lopsided in favor of the lenders and their increasing profits through interest payment on loaned surplus tends to maximize control over the consumer by maximizing the consumer's debt obligations. In a completely controlled economy such actions would lead to a landless poverty stricken labor class and an affluent class of lenders as overseers and owners of all land, resources and labor opportunities. In such a society surpluses are then produced for international trade only; seeking trade wealth from other nations, but purposely not expanding consumption in the native communities. Worker consumption is maintained at subsistence levels, while worker productivity is maximized at minimum cost for technology and training. Such a society would continue in physical despair for the poor and spiritual despair for the affluent indefinitely; for want of some environmental catastrophe or a convulsive revolution.

In an unstructured world economy, surpluses in one community are bartered for necessary goods that are surplus in other communities, on a cash (or direct barter) exchange basis; and over time there are no significant unused surpluses. People will produce what they and others will consume. There would be little or no lending and therefore little or no debt.

In a structured world economy where ownership, control of resources and control of labor opportunity are the economic model, surpluses are generally artificial, being available for consumption on credit for higher prices than would occur in a cash only economy. Wages are depressed below their true productivity value and workers are encouraged to purchase consumables on credit. Essentially the difference in wages paid and the true wage value of worker production is the source of profit for the company that will ultimately be loaned as credit to consumers to purchase the full wage value of goods and services produced in our economies.

The problem that arises for all such economies is that if the interest on loans comes out of productivity wages then consumers will not be able to purchase and consume all goods produced; because they will be servicing a debt (interest cost for past consumption on credit) in place of buying everything produced and desired; Our economies have found two ways that temporarily bypass this problem. First, additional credit is extended to workers to continue their year to year consumption; this simply results from the need to rollover profits from productivity to encourage consumption. Second, the quantity of money in circulation is always increasing so that the total interest charged for all loans, as a percentage of all productive labor dollars, will be created by the banking institutions and brought into the economy where it becomes the year to year inflation of costs for goods and services. The more debt in an economy and the higher the interest rates on that debt, the more inflation will increase for that economy. Increase both debt and interest costs on debt substantially and inflation will both accelerate and become economically destructive.

Inflation hurts everyone, but it tends to hurt lenders more; as long as wages increase to keep pace with inflation, debts are paid back with cheaper productivity wages. The very instrument of wage control, debt repaid with interest, is the instrument that produces the inflation that will lesson the debt. This is a continual dilemma for the financiers of debt. If interest rates are low they get little return on their loans, but inflation also remains low; if interest rates go up, so will their profits, but inflation will soon increase and profits will then be reduced by the decline in the value of the dollars being repaid. If wages do not keep up with inflation (wages become somewhat deflated), then such reduction in wages becomes an offset to interest-inflation. The overall interest on loans in our economy, less the overall reduction in productivity wages on a yearly basis, yields the net annual inflation of our economy.

Interest is a charge against the productivity of an economy. It either reduces wages below a stable neutral point or it increases the money supply above a stable neutral point. In either case, or a mix of both, prices increase for consumers and are reported as inflation. And all of this is done simply to control productivity, create debt, and allow a relatively small class of citizens to leach their needs for goods and services by controlling or owning resources, productivity, opportunity, and surpluses to create false debts upon which profits can be taken.

It seems paradoxical that the Federal Reserve bankers use increased interest rates to control inflation. Until we realize that the production and consumption modus operandi of our economy is so loaded with debt and so many companies and consumers are maxed-out on the amount they may borrow, that consumption can be reduced and thereby production also, by raising the cost to borrow sufficient to prevent many would-be consumers from being able to purchase everything being produced, causing manufacturers to lower prices and reduce production, leading to worker layoffs, which will also lead to reduced consumption. For the Federal Reserve to keep inflation at zero year-over-year, it must cause productivity losses to manufacturers, and wage losses to workers, equal to the amount of debt interest income of lenders that is created in the economy. The Federal Reserve simply assumes the role of the manufacturer and increases (inflates) the price of consumption such that consumers must reduce the amount of goods and services that they can afford to purchase on their relatively declining wage income. This is a real plus for bankers; the Federal Reserve controls inflation by the very mechanism that increases inflation; they just do it in such a way to cause income losses from the real productivity of the economy to balance their actions.

Chapter 7 - National Debt

When we borrow money in a social business sense, we must repay it to the lender; and we must also pay a fee for the use of that money, called interest. For most of us the money to repay our personal debts comes from our labor and it is relatively easy to associate our labor with the money we use to purchase things and repay debts. Hopefully we are learning that the money we are borrowing is the surplus labor of others that is made available to credit-worthy borrowers through banks and other forms of lending. So when we go into debt we are actually borrowing surplus labor from others, in order to purchase the goods and services and resources of still others. We want to consume now, but we have no surplus or stored labor available to exchange. So we promise to repay our debts with our future surplus labor or forfeit the stored labor of our other property and possessions, if we cannot repay.

Our government debt is not the same as our personal debt, because government does not raise funds by transforming raw materials into finished goods, or by bartering labor for labor. Government is funded by taking some of the labor of our economy as taxes, and by persuading others to lend surplus labor to the government, with promises of eventual repayment through taxes. Government does not have property and possessions to offer to those who have lent to it, outside of public lands and minerals. It only has the power to take future labor from those who labor productively or those who acquire surpluses by controlling such labor. Government cannot save for the future, for us as individuals, or collectively. Government spends for infrastructure and immediate consumption. Anything left over may only be used to reduce the following year's taxes or increase the current services to ourselves. So government debt is really a misfeasance in the way taxes are collected, a malfeasance in the way our taxes are spent, and a nonfeasance in the way we are protected from future tax burdens to repay that debt.

We hear a lot about the amount of debt accruing in the government sector, business sector, and the private consumer sector. Trillions of dollars of debt! Where did all this money come from? What manner of economy can generate such vast amounts of surplus labor wealth (consumable material goods and services), and yet tolerate such vast amounts of debt? Much of our public debt is long-term debt, which means that whatever principle sum we borrow, be it on the federal, state, or municipal level, we will pay far more in interest, than principal, to those with enough surplus resources to lend to governments. Our system enriches the very people that should be taxed to ensure that we would not have government debts. It would be interesting to know the sum of interest payments being made by all levels of government. The average working taxpayer might be appalled at the amount for which he and she are being milked and bilked.

It is very important for us to realize that debt can only happen when there is a surplus, because we can only borrow what is surplus. Trillions of dollars of debt arises from trillions of dollars of surplus productivity traded for immediate consumption. Our society is producing a very large surplus of goods and services and then encouraging the consumers of that surplus to go into debt to consume it. The amount of internal debt in any country is equal to the amount of surplus goods produced and consumed over and above a cash economy. Such debt reflects consumption controlled by disparity of incomes in that society.

Consider the U.S. national debt, pushing 89 trillion dollars in 2007. The government establishes a budget annually of a certain number of dollars. It also estimates the amount of taxes and fees that will come to it to pay the bills allocated in the budget. In a balanced budget the taxes and fees equal the bills to be paid. If there is a surplus of taxes, then either taxes can be reduced in the future, or additional services can be purchased for all. If there are more bills than tax dollars then the government is running a deficit and needs to raise taxes or reduce spending. Today, when there is a short-fall of taxes to pay our common bills, government is borrowing from the surplus rather than taxing the surplus, promising to tax our surplus in the future to pay back for today's consumption without taxation. What makes future surplus more taxable than today's surplus, considering that today's surplus is the only sure thing? The concept of taxing the common produce of the nation to provide for our common needs has been turned around to become the concept of reducing taxes and then borrowing what should be taken, and offering interest payments on those borrowings. The working class is taxed on their Income by government, taxed on their labor by their employer to provide profits, and then taxed by the government again to pay interest to the employers when they loan their profits to the government. Though we continually put off repayment of the principle of government debt by selling more bonds to cover for those coming due, we must pay the interest on that debt every year; and this payment comes from taxes collected by the Treasury every year. How nice for persons that can afford to own a debt, which in a truly democratic society of equal representation they would have been taxed on their excessive income to avoid such debts.

Congress has the authority to take whatever it deems necessary from the surplus of today to do our public business. It makes no sense for government to take by force a portion of every worker's labor as taxes and also borrow from those who have such a surplus that they are willing to loan it to government. It is a defect in government to borrow at any time, since government has the authority to tax the surplus labor of the present, which is the only source of income available to government and ourselves. When government borrows from today's surplus rather than take that surplus through taxation, it is consuming the same surplus in either case. The private economy is not disparaged less by borrowing than it is by taxation. Consumption is consumption. What the government consumes is not available to the private economy, no matter how the government came by it. But the obligation to pay interest yearly on that debt, and the obligation to someday repay the principal of the debt, is a criminal conspiracy between our politicians and the debt financiers. With proper taxation there is no interest or principle.

The national debt has in the past always ballooned during periods of war. The government issues bonds to those who have a surplus of labor and resources, rather than raise taxes. A double whammy occurs at this point to balloon that debt, when the government spends the money received in the sale of bonds, to purchase materials and supplies to carry on a war. While the same people who buy those bonds, control the resources and industries that make the goods used to conduct wars. And these people have always raised prices and profiteered from such national emergencies. Even those who capitalize a war industry out of their own pockets, appearing to sacrifice for the good of the nation, have only done so when they have a contract in hand that guarantees them a return on their surplus, much higher than a peacetime economy would have afforded them. So the sellers of goods have a hand in providing the means for government to purchase war goods at a price set by the producers, based on the necessity of having those goods to protect the nation. War does not reinforce freedom; it reinforces the control over resources and opportunities, and the future labor value of workers, to benefit those owners of industry. War debts are phony debts, wherein a few profit while many sacrifice.

A form of anarchy has replaced the representative democracy that used to reign in America.
Though our government has important and legitimate needs, it refuses to tax our economy even when we have sufficient labor and resources to pay our bills directly without the need to borrow. This political crime is aggravated by making the interest payment of the government debt, the only item in the national budget that cannot be reduced, or abolished, while all other expenditures can be reduced or abolished. The fact is, the surplus is there or there would be nothing to be borrowed. And if all government income must come from surplus that exists today, why is part raised by taxes and part by borrowing, if not to enrich those who are already enriched by owning the surplus of our economy, at the expense of the laborer and the poor?

We must begin to view the national debt as a problem for the present, rather than something that began in the past and can be put off until some time in the future. The income that government receives in taxes comes only from our current productivity, because the past is spent and the future is unknown, both in terms of government needs and dollars that will be available. Therefore there are no past taxes or future taxes to oppress us. Likewise, there is no past national debt or future national debt to burden us. But there is a current tax burden and debt burden that we must finance daily, weekly, and monthly. Since we carry this burden every day and service this debt from our current productive labor, it is a problem for the present. It can never be a problem for the future, and should not be viewed in a way that makes us believe we are postponing an expense from today until some time in the future. Whether government taxes us or borrows from today's surplus, it is receiving and using current dollars, paying current bills and current interest on current debt.

If the injury to society is improper taxation, the insult is the interest paid to those who have a surplus to begin with. Interest is not a reward for civic duty, nor should it be looked upon as an entitlement program for banks, businesses, and the wealthy. As the debt grows it requires more and more interest to service it. This has the potential of deepening the divisions between our socio-economic classes by forcing some citizens to pay ever-increasing amounts of their labor to government, while government just transfers much of that labor to the lenders.

Consider that while our federal debt is over nine trillion dollars, our states, counties, and cities are collectively trillions more in debt. They also borrow from today's surplus to finance many projects. They sell bonds to raise money and agree to raise taxes in the future to pay back those bonds, with a competitive rate of interest. But these are just many more cases of borrowing from today's surplus instead of taxing. Those dollars are paid in the present and near past for goods and services that were available for our consumption, or we would not have those debts. Add to those public debts our private corporate and consumer debts that now exceed forty trillion dollars, and we realize that today's consumption of today's production is neither Communistic nor Democratic. Only pyramids of

Oligarchy Capitalism, or stratified classes of Fascism, can control the cost of today's production to own the personal and communal debts of today's workers.

With a national domestic product of ten trillion dollars per year and a combined public and private debt over sixty trillion dollars, we have managed to promise the payment of six years of our total future productivity to somebody. Most indentures of servitude were set at seven years in Colonial times. Six years of total servitude in this "new age" is definitely out of bounds. And when you consider that only labor can pay a debt, the 100 million full time workers in our economy are each on the hook for an average $600,000 dollars of our public and private debt. If all of the interest paid on all debts averaged five percent annually, then the average worker pays $30,000 dollars per year in interest out of their labor on that total debt.

Interest on debt is a wage cut. The more interest you pay the less labor you have to barter for goods. When we take out a loan for $1000, and agree to pay back $1100 over twelve months, we are giving ourselves a wage cut of $100 for one year in order to consume today. We could save our labor for a year and consume later when we would only have to barter our labor for the labor value of the goods we desire. Interest on loans is labor. It does not increase the cost of goods; rather it decreases the barter value of our labor by laying claim to our future labor until the loan is paid. The interest on the national debt is a wage cut for all who pay taxes. If the annual interest on the national debt is 300 billion dollars, being paid by 100 million workers, then the average person is paying $3,000 annually out of their wages to the owners of that debt. Government appears equally able to increase wealth for some by cutting their taxes or cutting the wages of our labor force and giving the proceeds as interest-labor to the debt holders. This wage cut occurs year after year and will continue into the future. The laborers' standard of living is declining because many must have less so that the debt financiers may have more.

The hidden dagger, ever threatening to dismember our society and leave many of the ill and aged to fend for themselves, is the interest on the National Debt. The interest due on the National Debt is the only government expenditure that cannot be cut, altered, or abolished. All other expenditures can be completely eliminated, if necessary, to provide tax funds to pay this obligation. If the interest rate averages 5%, then it will cost 450 billion dollars per year to maintain this 9-trillion dollar debt annually. If the interest rate should rise to 10%, then it will cost 900 billion per year to maintain it. Consider that for 2006, government income was about 2.3 trillion dollars, and the deficit for fiscal 2006 was about 300 billion dollars, making a 2006 federal budget of 2.6 trillion dollars. If taxes paid to government six or seven years down the road were the same as in 2006, it would only require interest rates of 25% on the nine-plus trillion-dollar national debt to consume all government income from taxes just to pay the interest due. There would be no money for Social Security, Medicare, national defense, government pensions, roads and bridges, schools, etc., without borrowing 100% of our annual needs; an incredibly scary prospect. And we are assured by most economists and economic forecasters that the National Debt will continue to increase in the future, simply because we borrow from the surplus of today when we should tax.

Keep in mind that the nine-plus trillion-dollar U.S. national debt represents the principle of loans to purchase and consume nine-plus trillion dollars worth of goods and services. Such that after we have consumed what is bought we then owe the lenders that amount, nine-plus trillion and rising. While we pay an enormous yearly interest bill to keep those lenders from demanding repayment.

These trillions upon trillions of dollars of debt represent untold years of productive labor of millions to produce goods and services. That productive labor is done. The goods have been manufactured, distributed, and consumed. So why all of this consumption debt? We live together on the Earth, we labor with its resources, and we consume its bounty. We may only use what exists, eat what grows, live in dwellings made from environmental materials. We cannot eat debt, shelter ourselves with it, heal the sick with it, or provide for our future with it. Debt serves no purpose but to divide society by oppressing and denying the liberties, equalities, and responsibilities of creation. The upper class owns the debt and profits by it, while the lower class appears to owe that debt and is forced to service it year by year. This is forced servitude that is contrary to our entire moral and political heritage.

Chapter 8 - Deficits and Taxes

Is it possible for government to have a budget deficit? On the surface it would seem so; budget deficits seem obvious, not to mention persistent. A slightly deeper look into the machinations of funding government (the most public of corporations), reveals that there is no such thing as a deficit, nor is there such a thing as a national debt. A government that oversees a productive and profitable economy, and which has legitimate costs to do its duties, must tax that productivity to pay for its expenses. To take less than what it needs from our national productivity and yet borrow from that same productivity, offering the profit of interest to the lenders, along with burdens of debt to the producing laborers, is a conspiracy to defraud and enslave the working class.

Government must pay its bills, and the money used to pay those bills can only be, and are in fact, tax dollars. There are no other dollars available to a government unless it simply creates them, which is taxation by inflation, devaluing future labor until wages rise to consume those dollars. The definition of debt is, in principle, the obligation to repay borrowed labor or borrowed commodities, from one person to another, or from one group of persons to another. But no person or group of persons can be in debt to themselves. Only a moron would take money from his wallet to spend on himself, and replace it with an IOU. We are in principle supposed to be one people, indivisible. We cannot be in debt to ourselves; we cannot write ourselves an IOU. Therefore, the so-called national debt is not a debt. It is, however, misfeasance and malfeasance in the operation of government.

So how can these borrowed deficit dollars be considered taxes? Quite simply it follows from the force or persuasion principle, which is the principle by which all levels of society interact with government. We are all familiar with the power of government to force our participation in the tax system. The government also takes in tax dollars through persuasion. This is accomplished by having the elected representatives create a Government Investment Program (GIP), whose function is to take seed money from the dollars coming in by force and offer it as interest payments to anyone persuaded to invest money in the government. The Government Investment Program is competing for, and getting, surplus dollars from many private investment groups, such as insurance companies, mutual funds companies, retirement funds, large and small businesses and corporations, all manner of stocks and bonds related investment companies, foreign companies and citizens, foreign governments, etc. Since individuals own all manner of corporations by owning stock in those companies, all of these persuasion tax dollars are idle dollars held by individuals, who are directly, or through their elected corporate representatives, or through their hired investment counselors, seeking to put those dollars on loan to increase their future wealth at labor's expense.

Much of the idle wealth accumulated in the 1980's came as a result of tax reform, whereby taxes were reduced for everyone. However, upper income citizens reaped greater amounts of wealth to re-invest, while the federal government was running larger and larger fictitious deficits. With wealthy individuals and corporations already taking substantial labor rewards from their workers, government services would have to be cut or government would have to raise funds another way. Borrowing idle dollars from wealth was chosen. But since our government is supposed to be a non-profit organization, every dollar coming in is spent, and since our government is also supposed to be a non-debt organization, every dollar taken in by persuasion, must eventually be repaid with a dollar taken in by force, plus interest. Persuasion taxes on idle wealth will be converted to forced taxes on the productive workers.

If a person labors day in and day out, and his or her labor is bartered in the marketplace, we accept that the employer is entitled to a share of that labor value, likewise the federal government, the state governments, and the local governments. All is well and good, except when we find that those who profit from the labor of others, over and above their own labor, are then able to lend that surplus to the government and reap more of the future labor of those who have no surplus labor to provide a similar benefit unto themselves.

110

Persuasion tax money is idle money, and is not needed by wealth to expand the private economy. The economy would not suffer if all taxes were forced taxes, and it would be perceived to be much stronger because there would never be an artificial deficit.

Although banks must keep a certain amount of their depositors' dollars in reserve, available to cover withdrawal demands and to pay for insurance from the government on all deposits, using the government's liquidity to cover for any mismanagement by the banks. The GIP does not retain any reserves against the spending of these persuasion dollars except the printing press to create new dollars, the power to raise additional taxes by force, and the power to sell national resources (parks, lands, minerals, forests, etc.) to the debt holders. In our current fiscal difficulties the government must keep the seven trillion dollars taken in by the GIP in an idle state simply because government is still forced to continue persuading additional idle dollars to be deposited into the GIP.

What is becoming ridiculous is the cost of keeping all those spent dollars from being returned to the investors. The Government Investment Program must compete with private investment companies, national and international, to retain those trillions of investor dollars. Its only power to do so lies in offering higher interest returns, and the fear of the consequences to international economics if the investors fail to leave these idle dollars where they are. Since these dollars are already spent, any request for withdrawal of the principle by investors in the GIP that could not be repaid by additional borrowing from other investors would have to be raised by the confiscation of private assets. In other words, government would have to raise forced taxes drastically to pay persuasion tax refunds, so that those least able to pay would have to contribute to refunds for those most able to pay.

The on-going tug-of-war between idle wealth and the producing class makes our social existence very precarious. Those who hold the paper of government debt should be advised that when the producing class is no longer able or willing to service that debt, the government will be obligated to raise the taxes of those most able to pay, in order to pay off these notes. It would be the easiest way to abrogate a debt that is not a debt and should never have occurred in the first place. So if government fails to take in the first place, what it spends in the first place, then those who have been persuaded to invest in government will come to realize that they have also been taken. Such is the reality of the taxation authority that resides in the people.

The federal government and the people are two different entities now. Since the people have already paid their taxes, the federal government will have to turn to its controllers to abrogate this debt. Keep in mind that the interest expense on the national debt is paid to keep the nine-plus trillion dollar principal from coming due. When those who invest in these pieces of paper determine that our eroded job base does not have enough taxable income to support our own needs, as well as the interest expense on their bond-paper, they will cash in those bonds as they mature, adding additional hundreds of billions of dollars to our tax burdens yearly. And you can be assured that not only will your taxes go up, but also the cost of Medicare, Medicaid, Food Stamps, Social Security, Head Start. Many other programs will be cut or abolished to help pay back those bonds. The choices for the future are to pay the bills and suffer social chaos while maintaining economic stability; or do not pay the bills and suffer economic chaos, while trying to maintain social stability. Or inflate the currency, pay the bills with worthless dollars, and bring on both economic and social chaos.

Many believe our country can operate with an unbalanced budget, when in fact we have always had a balanced budget. We just use unbalanced taxation to achieve it, borrowing from idle wealth directly and through its myriad investment resources, to cover our government's obligations to ourselves. A balanced budget amendment is a farcical thing, since every budget is always balanced (forced taxes and persuasion taxes equal money spent). A new amendment should be called "the equitable and forced taxation from all" amendment.

Does the middle class really believe that their pension funds, mutual funds, and life insurance money can be invested in government bonds to provide future income for themselves, without requiring that they tax themselves into poverty to pay those bonds when they are due; or requiring that their money inflate to worthless paper? Labor barters for labor and consumption privileges today. The future can only be likewise. If you expect to receive a pension when you retire, and your pension fund is investing in government bonds, then you should prepare yourself to continue working until death retires you. You will have to pay your share of the increasing taxes that will come due to pay all of the bonds that we the government owe to ourselves.

The argument by some politicians and some economists that we need not force the up-front collections of all money to be spent by government through forced taxation is ludicrous. A trillion dollars paid out in interest money in President Reagan's years to expand and maintenance this pool of idle dollars is morally and economically criminal. Another trillion dollars in interest was paid out in the first President Bush's term. And even more in President Clinton's term; and still more in the terms of Bush-2. If we cannot pay our bills in relative good times, we shall not survive as a nation in the worst of times.

Yet the political buffoons will increase Social Security taxes every year, (which is not only paid by each laborer but is matched dollar for dollar by the employer), spending a significant portion of these dollars off-budget to help finance government. All the while telling us that they are investing the surplus Social Security taxes for our future. How could dollars spent for today's consumption be considered an investment that can be refunded to pay for future consumption? That money is gone forever. This process is just another worthless IOU from us to us.

Social Security as disability or pension income will be bankrupt in ten to twenty years. The surplus Social Security taxes taken in today are traded for treasury notes and bonds, redeemable in the form of income taxes in the future. When the federal government will be unable to tax income to pay the ever-growing interest on the national debt, it will also be unable to tax income to pay back the bonds purchased by the Social Security trust funds. The purchasing of government bonds is no longer an investment. The approaching impossibility of repaying those investments, or the interest on them, makes them a give-away, or donation to government.

Government can never be a good investment in a capitalist economy. The whole principle of democracy and its relationship to an economy is that the government would tax, spend, and regulate both personal and corporate productivity to provide for our common needs, to promote our continued prosperity, and to always maintain a net asset wealth of infrastructure owned by all and free of debt. Government takes what we need; it cannot ethically borrow in the sense of mortgaging our future. Workers are paid weekly, BI-weekly, or monthly, and corporations calculate their profits monthly and quarterly. So there is no reason why government cannot establish monthly tax payments from labor to pay its monthly bills. If necessary, the government could establish different fiscal years for different workers and corporations to smooth over seasonal and other income aberrations. There is no reason why government should not have 100 to 200 billion dollars available to cover for any natural disasters until taxes can be adjusted to pay any new expenses. But there should never be a deficit or national debt.

Nine trillion dollars invested by private citizens and foreigners, in government spending needs, show where the trickle-down economies got sidetracked. When President Reagan lowered taxes to promote investment in business and entrepreneurship, he should also have lowered interest rates that the government would pay for private money, to ensure that the reduced taxes on the wealthy would cause them to invest their surplus into expanding the private economy. Instead, government had to raise interest rates, to compete with private enterprise, to borrow the money needed to fund government, since spending was increased after taxes were reduced. For many years government has been a safe and profitable investment for the very dollars it should have taken to pay for government spending. It is impossible for government to be a wealth-producing investment, unless it is also a poverty-producing indenture. We are one people; therefore, if some can

114

increase their wealth by mortgaging our common needs, then many others must increase their poverty to pay that mortgage.

The portion of these deposits in the government that is owned by retirement funds, insurance companies, states and municipalities, demonstrates a collective belief that you can give yourself an IOU. If government takes or accepts money contributed by these above named groups, giving them the IOU promise, then government will be obligated at some point in the future to persuade if not coerce these groups to contribute those moneys a second time. The interest paid to these groups to keep them in the scam is approaching the character of a Ponzi scheme, (using new investment money to pay previous investors dividends, to attract more investment until the operator of the scheme takes as much as he can and disappears before it all collapses). When government runs out of legitimate investors, it will begin using the electronic printing press to pay the profits expected by earlier depositors, because it cannot disappear. And finally, the portion of these deposits invested by foreign individuals and foreign governments demonstrates some gross errors in commerce, when the most powerful, most productive, and largest economy in the world, cannot conduct international trade for a net surplus of dollars. It is instead forced or persuaded to conduct trade in such a manner that the profits made by foreign companies and governments come back as investments in our domestic spending requirements. Either for want of a more lucrative investment or for political power to maintain the unfortunate circumstances which have created and which sustain these exported profits.

We are failing as a community to deal fairly with each other. Those who store their wealth in pieces of paper, issued by governments, should know that labor is bartered for labor, and those who harvest a bumper crop today cannot set it aside for the future in pieces of paper. People will not always be property and laborers will not always be slaves; those who wish to own the future will find that their paper wealth will be abrogated. If we are going to continue to tax the lower class with lack of opportunity, the middle class by force, and the upper class by persuasion, giving the persuaded first feeding at the communal trough, then we are a short way from self destruction. Bad taxation policies should not make good investments for surplus dollars. Posterity has the right of self-determination and cannot be sold into slavery for today's folly. Since it is doubtful that our children will accept this debt as theirs, and also doubtful that the debt will be forgiven, we have only social strife and the threat of revolution to dog us, until we are captives of its violent processes.

Eventually, foreigners investing in our economy and our government debt will need their money to support their own economies. We will either destroy our currency if we print those dollars for them, or we will destroy our economy if we are forced to tax ourselves to raise the capital necessary to repay such bonds; or we will sell our resources to them and become economically dominated like South America and Africa.

The Earth is free, when honored; sufficient, when shared; abundant, when sacrificed for. Let those who fence off the Earth's resources be aware, the laborers who are being farmed for profit by the capitalist aristocracy, and saddled with public debt, bankrupting their economic and social future, will not be legally obligated to pay this bondage.

Government cannot be in debt, nor can it have deficits in the budget process. We are one people, and we pay our bills with tax dollars collected by ourselves. Whether we choose to tax and spend or borrow and spend, we are paying those bills with dollars collected by the Treasury Department, and if the Treasury wants to switch the country from forced taxation to one of persuasion taxation, so be it. Wealth and political power are often inseparable, and this marriage is just as often unavoidable. I call upon the persons of wealth and influence to bring their considerable powers to bear upon the federal government to either reduce expenditures to the level of tax income immediately, or to bring their considerable powers to bear upon their wealth, and force the government to take from them, without obligation to refund, those moneys which were idly invested in treasury notes, to balance the federal budget. If you do not help the nation voluntarily to the benefit and preservation of all, the working class will help themselves later, to your specific detriment. You

116

are fiscally irresponsible to disregard the consequences, in your pursuit of personal gain, just as the lower classes are irresponsible in demanding expenditures of borrowed funds, without regard to those same consequences. Let's not be GIP'ed out of our future.

Chapter 9 - Banks

Banks have been around in one form or another for hundreds of years. Early banks were usually individual merchants who needed people with surplus products that they wanted to sell, and other people with other surplus products that they would be willing to barter and trade through the merchant for foreign goods. Still another group of people would borrow surplus goods that the merchant could sell by contract on credit, paying back more than they borrowed from future harvests or labor. The merchant profited from the margin created by charging more than he paid for any commodity. In a community or in a nation, this is the foundation of banking. Banks are the chief outlets for us to store, exchange, and borrow that universal labor receipt we call money.

Who is the largest borrower in the U.S.? The government appears to win hands down, but it is not the largest borrower. The banking system is the largest borrower by far. We think of banks as lenders and as a place to store our surplus labor-money. But like government, banks do not create real money; their greatest source of money to lend, is borrowed money. Banks make their profit by charging more for the use of the money that they lend, than they pay to borrow it from depositors. So where do the banks get their loans? From people and businesses that put money in savings accounts and checking accounts. Laborers and businesses are the biggest and primary lenders in our economy, because they are the only source of labor, both stored and surplus. Banks are only secondary lenders, because they are borrowing from the surplus of our productive labors, which we deposit in them to be loaned to others. When a bank pays interest for our cash and check deposits, it is borrowing those deposits from those who have a surplus over and above their current needs. Without this type of surplus, banks would go out of business immediately. And banks do go out of business during recessions and depressions when there is no surplus labor for them to borrow.

A bank must loan as much of the labor money that

it has borrowed as the banking regulations will allow, in order to maximize the amount of interest income it will receive, to pay bills and make a profit. Bank regulations require that some money be kept in reserve to give back to depositors wishing to withdraw their money. Competition between banks forces them to offer higher returns to depositors when they need to borrow more, and to offer lower loan rates of interest to their customers when they have extra money to loan. The correct relationship of a bank to its community is that when you deposit money in a savings or checking account you are the lender (the banker) and the bank is your customer (the borrower), paying you for the use of your surplus money. When a bank makes a loan, it becomes the lender; and the borrower is their customer, paying them for the use of the money that is actually borrowed from you and I. Banks want us to feel that they are giving us a service when we loan them our surplus labor-money, and then want us to feel that they are also giving us something when we take out a loan. In neither case is the bank giving anyone anything; they are doing business, earning a profit by renting-out surplus labor at a higher price than they pay to borrow it. The banker is just a middleman in the commerce of laborers bartering with other laborers to use our surplus. However, they have gotten the politicians and especially the Federal Reserve to create laws and regulations that protect banks from failure at public expense. This places the Federal Reserve and bankers as middlemen in control of commerce and economic opportunity. They are the choke point of all of our economic enterprises because they control the movement of our surplus and stored labor.

The current competition among banks and their past relationship to their communities is changing drastically. We used to have two types of banks in the United States. Small community banks received their deposits from their local community and only made loans in their local community. The other type were larger state and national banks, which received funds from big business and taxes taken in by government, and which made loans to big business and to governments. The small banks are disappearing. The regulation, deregulation, and re-regulation of banks has caused our current banking industry to focus on mergers and buyouts to the point where very few community banks remain independently owned. Today most deposits go into large pools of money held by large banking corporations. Those deposits seldom remain in the community. So if you need a loan you are competing with all other borrowers in the nation (and even the world) to get your bank to loan you money.

Loan rates do not reflect the economic conditions in your community like they did in the past. In the past when economic activity was slow and businesses were not borrowing, a bank would lower its loan rates to encourage more borrowing. And they would likewise pay less interest to depositors, which would encourage some to seek to get a larger return by starting a business or expand their current businesses with their own funds. In either case business expansion would occur in the local community. If a community is in recession today, bankers need not try to loan their money at lower interest rates in their community. They will simply transfer that money to other areas of the country where loan rates are higher. This keeps the economically depressed community in recession longer, while the banks use locally deposited money to make a bigger profit for themselves and make areas of strong economic activity even stronger.

Since banks do not create money, but do act as a conduit to move that surplus labor to areas where it will be consumed, the amount of money in circulation is very important to banks. Several things must occur in an economy for money to reflect the activity of that economy. There must be sufficient dollars to equal the value of the productive labor ongoing in the economy; additional dollars to reflect the savings in the bank or in our pockets, for recent past labor; and still other dollars to reflect the present economic value of stored labor in goods, or factories and farms, infrastructure, etc. Although banks are still a very important component in our economy, they should not be allowed to drive the economy, or to conspire with resource owners to abuse labor, from whom they both profit. Government must regulate banks for the benefit of the laborers who create money with their labor.

Banks also have a banking system that they

deposit some of our money in and borrow from. Their banking system is called the Federal Reserve System. Banks are regulated both by federal law and the Federal Reserve System. They must hold certain amounts of our money in reserve, deposited in a Federal Reserve Bank, of which there are twelve. Outside of regulated reserves, banks may lend their depositors' money to individuals, companies, other banks, all levels of government, or even invest it in other markets and other nations. Banks are somewhat subject to economic controls on how they invest or lend our money, because the Federal Reserve can raise or lower interest rates, which banks may receive on deposits or pay on loans that they have in a Federal Reserve Bank. If the bankers in control of the Federal Reserve want to slow down the economy, they increase interest rates on bank deposits in the Federal Reserve System. This encourages banks to keep more of our money on loan to the Federal Reserve and unavailable to loan to businesses and individuals. Less exchange money means less efficient labor exchange, which slows our economic activity. By lowering interest rates paid to banks on their Federal Reserve deposits, the Fed encourages banks to withdraw deposits and offer that money to business and industry at loan rates that will expand our economy by creating jobs to produce more goods and services.

Banks must maintain capital reserves of different amounts on different types of loans they make, against the possible losses the banks would suffer on defaulted loans. At least 8% of the amount a bank lends for industrial and commercial loans must be held in reserve. For Federally insured home loans, just under 2% must be held in reserve. For investment by banks in Treasury Bonds, no reserve is required. So if a bank wants to minimize risk and maximize profits, it puts its money in the market with the least reserve requirements. It sets loan rates for home loans slightly higher to equal the returns available from Government money, considering the reserves that must be held. And in the case of commercial loans, which can generate jobs and surplus labor, the banks may either make no money available or charge such high rates and set such punitive requirements that industry and business are forced to postpone expansion, research and development; while they are encouraged by the marketplace to seek funds overseas. Even to the point of moving manufacturing jobs out of the country to gain foreign investment capital or to compete with other businesses that have already made the move. When bank loans become scarce for business and industry, expect a recession; if mortgage money also becomes scarce, expect a deep recession.

Though we value banks for their willingness to borrow our surplus, and pay us a dividend for the use of our surplus, their existence and continuance stems strictly from the concept of debt. Without private debt, banking would be meaningless and non-existent. In an absolutely free market banks would still profit from our debt structure, but they would not control it. In our actual controlled economy, which is not a free market, banks are allies of big business and often conspire to expand or restrict industries, communities, and other country's economies when it is profitable for them and their associate capitalists to do so. Banks provide leverage to industry to work against the very laborers whose labor provides 100% of the bank's deposits. And in the last few years they have even taken to profiteering from all large and small transactions going on in our economy; from the writing of a check, to the use of a credit card or a cash machine. All transfers of money for purposes of consumption are now taxed by the banking industry, much of which is foreign owned, to continue raising record profits for those owners. The laborer is controlled economically more today than the previous several generations. He or she is working more for less and will have to work longer years to maintain their subsistence, while fees and hidden bank taxes will continue to reduce the laborer's standard of living.

Chapter 10 - Gold and Silver

The lust for gold and silver throughout history is a part of the plot of a great number of books and movies. These metals are worshipped as much as any icon of wood, stone, iron or imagination. The gold icons of one culture have often been stolen and recast into the gold icons of another culture.

Besides being used in objects of worship, art and jewelry; gold and silver have long been used as a store of value to exchange goods, wherein the buyer used gold or silver to trade for consumable goods and services. This store of value has become the definition of idle wealth, the desire of every person to be able to consume life's necessities without having to labor to produce them.

There are many ways that a society can use and control a commodity like gold or silver as a medium of exchange. For example, imagine a growing agricultural based community wherein the surplus goods of each family is brought to a centralized market and exchanged through bartering for the goods of others. The problem that arises in this situation is that many will not bring their surplus, or may not invest their labor throughout the year to produce a surplus, if it is unlikely that they will need what others have to offer. The ability for a society to maximize productive effort, and the trading that would be associated with that effort, requires that a purchaser may obtain surplus goods for future use and consumption; separate from his or her bartering the products of their labor; and that a seller may sell surplus goods and services without immediately purchasing any specific consumable items in return. There are two principle ways to accomplish this. One is for a seller to receive a promissory note allowing him or her to demand certain goods and services associated with those notes at sometime in the future or to trade those notes to others in exchange for notes associated with other goods and services. Of course the problems of counterfeiting promissory notes, or a situation where those who were obligated to fulfill a note with a specific commodity or service could not do so, would tend to hamper that form of economic activity and growth. The other way to establish an efficient exchange of goods is to use a durable commodity of limited supply, such as gold, to be a store of value associated with the goods and services of productive labor. It can be used as an exchange medium in a manner where those who want to sell their surplus, but do not want to purchase any goods, could barter their surplus for gold, hold it for any length of time, and eventually trade it for any other desired goods or services. The universality of using gold and silver as exchange money easily displaced promissory notes where sufficient gold was available to promote economic activity. Our modern paper money is actually a combination of the universal exchange of gold and the set value associated with promissory notes.

The use of gold as money was not without problems and limitations. To use gold as an exchange medium requires the production of coins and or bars made of pure gold or alloys of gold and other metal. The possibility of producing counterfeit coins by not having any gold in the alloy or by reducing the amount of gold below the stated value, would when discovered cause the current holder of that bad money to lose the purchasing power associated with the gold that should have been there. Another problem for gold, which often led to some governments' reducing the amount of gold in their standard coinage, was that there was not always enough gold or silver available to maintain a robust economy as well as to facilitate the money needs of an expanding economy. For gold and silver to be used as money and to remain relatively stable value, the amount in circulation must be equivalent to the amount of productive labor available for exchange. If people need to barter their labor goods using coinage such as gold and silver, then as surplus goods increase through increased productive labor or bountiful crops, additional gold and silver must be supplied to represent that labor; or price stability will be replaced with deflation. The flipside of increased production is of course decreased production, wherein war, weather, or disease may leave very few goods and services available, while demand is great. Prices on limited goods and services will inflate to consume the relative over-supply of gold and silver.

In times of unrest governments often taxed their citizenry to fight wars of national defense or wars of colonial conquest, removing gold and silver from their economy to pay for weapons and soldiers salaries, without realizing that it was the most important tool that their social economies used to produce the surpluses that allowed wars of defense and conquest to be undertaken. In times of peace, the bounty of the Earth or the vagary of failed harvests would cause coinage to accumulate in nations that had surpluses; coming from nations that were in need of goods. Nations with shortages are forced to trade gold in place of goods and services, until their gold ran out. While a nation with surplus goods available for trade would begin to hoard gold that was not needed to sustain its economy, or which during bad times would be hoarded by landowners through rents, or the government through taxes. Many economies were constantly stifled in growth and technical advancement, even with continuing years of abundance, because the limited amount of gold and silver available to represent the productive labor of an economy was hoarded and held as self-insurance against future bad harvests or other calamity. Generally throughout history too little gold or silver was available to promote risk taking and investment in producing surplus goods and expanding trade. This hoarded gold and silver was not available as capital where it could create economic opportunity and growth. It could only purchase the surplus of others in times of shortage, which might maintain a community or a nation until the gold ran out or local surpluses resumed, but it did not promote economic growth. Surpluses must remain in a community or be bartered for the surpluses of others, to allow growth in population and technical advances to take place. The hoarding of gold and silver is equivalent to it not existing and therefore not available to promote resource and labor exchange, as far as the local or national economy is concerned. The use of promissory notes has probably done more than gold or silver in expanding production and consumption in the last 800 years.

The problem of supply and demand for gold to expand commerce worldwide, and the need to have a stable exchange medium to allow the borrowing of money to hurt neither the borrower nor the creditor, has made it impossible to maintain a World monetary gold standard. There simply is not enough gold available to support international trade. Nor is their sufficient gold or silver to allow even the United States to establish money backed by gold and silver. This does not mean that in times of crisis gold and silver are of no economic benefit. On the contrary, in times of economic crisis only the limited amounts of these metals can provide a trustworthy conduit of exchange to rebuild a limited economy. In a crisis, paper money multiplies (inflates), debt income evaporates, unemployment increases, tax rates go up while government income from taxes shrinks; and devaluing assets are liquidated in exchange for consumables. Only the limited quantity of commodities like gold and silver, which can promote the creation of surplus production, can bring about new opportunities and expand an economy back to prosperity.

Today and throughout history gold miners force the goods and services markets to adjust in two ways, when they labor to increase the amount of money in the marketplace. First, because miners need goods and services to live on, which they purchase with new gold; hence, there are less goods and services available to be bartered amongst the laborers that produced those goods. This would seem trivial until we identify all of those whose labor is really just seeking gold and nothing else as compared to the cost of maintaining such pursuits. The second adjustment for the marketplace involves absorbing the new gold into the price structure. When the miners remove goods and services from the world's closed economy, they use new gold that must now continue to circulate in the economy. So those who traded goods or services to gold miners must now exchange that new gold for the goods and services they desire. And so it will roll over and over in the economy. But since it represents extra gold competing to purchase limited goods and services, prices will inflate until a new equilibrium price structure is in place; wherein the new level of gold circulating will promote a new level of stable prices for goods and services coming into the marketplace. Since all productive laborers are sellers in the marketplace, wages will also rise, since increased prices are the increased wages for laborers. In essence, the labor of gold seekers accomplishes nothing but their welfare at other laborers' expense, and the inflation of prices by the percentage of increased gold in their economy. The goods and services they consume are removed from possible consumption by others, and the money they bring is simply absorbed in trading that in the long run neither benefits nor greatly oppresses productive laborers by its presence.

Just a short example of how this works. Consider northern California in 1849 and early 1850's, after gold was discovered. Before this discovery prices were fairly stable for goods all across the country, with the exception that the costs to transport goods added to their price. When gold was suddenly very plentiful in California, and goods and services were fairly scarce, the prices on goods and services rose to consume the available gold. If a miner got his gold with very little effort, and if he felt he could obtain more after his current holdings were spent, he valued his gold less and parted with it in exchange for food, clothes, tools, and comfort, much more freely than people in other parts of the country. Since gold can only act as a medium of exchange, having a lot of gold in an economy with limited goods and services, means prices will inflate until the gold available establishes a new equilibrium of labor value, or is dispersed throughout the nation and eventually the world. Consider that in the gold fields, during the gold rush, a night in a hotel and a bath and breakfast could cost ten dollars in gold. One hundred miles away the same services would be only a few dollars and five hundred miles away one dollar in gold would purchase those same services. The same services are being exchanged in each local economy, but the amount of gold exchanged simply reflects the amount of gold available to each local economy. Increase the gold and prices will rise to consume it, decrease the gold available and prices will fall until trading continues. Goods and services trade for goods and services, and the medium of exchange can only reflect a relationship wherein prices allow the amount of exchange money available to equally represent all goods and services available.

So if we cannot operate our economy on a gold standard, what standard will work? Right now we are on a Federal Reserve Note standard, commonly called the dollar; in essence they are promissory notes wherein the promise is only a guarantee that they are spendable anywhere in our economy, not a promise to exchange them for gold or silver as they used to be. Our paper money is not backed by any commodity such as gold, and certainly not by the full faith and credit of the U.S. Government as we are told. Rather, <u>our American Dollar is backed only by the labor of American Workers</u>, and limiting the quantity of dollars in circulation controls the value of the dollar in relation to our national productivity. Considering our current population and the amount of economic activity that needs to occur to keep our economy healthy and expanding, we must have a large work force engaged in productive labor. A labor standard is the only money standard that can create a stable economy.

To demonstrate that gold and silver are at this time separated from their historic role as a store of value, consider that for the last several years, gold consumption has been greater than new production and recycling combined. The same is true for silver; industrial consumption is higher than all mining and reclaiming. This is occurring in a world where the population is growing faster than two percent a year; and where standards of living are increasing worldwide. Lack of understanding of the relationship of gold and silver to general economic transactions, has in essence reburied these metals, in hopes that they may never again be used or needed as the fundamental currencies of labor exchange.

As a standard in the past, a country's paper currency, treasury bonds and bills, and other notes had their values stipulated in quantities of gold. And through this mechanism each country's currency could be related to any other country's currency, creating fairly stable exchange rates that promoted trade and economic expansion. It also insulated a country's internal currency from trade pressure, because trade deficits were paid in gold that the creditor nation could spend in any country, not just the country from which the gold was received. In late 1969 gold was abandoned

130

as international trade money and countries stopped transferring gold to pay their trade debts. By then silver was also removed as a standard for domestic money in the industrialized world. Today the U.S. dollar has replaced gold as the medium of foreign exchange. So Gold and Silver are effectively de-monetized in our economies.

Even though gold and silver are in short supply and little used as money, the U.S. paper dollar is the wrong barometer of economic stability. Assets and commodities should not be valued in terms of dollars, but in terms of fixed quantity commodities like gold and silver. The unstable item (dollar) fluctuates in terms of the stable (gold), not vice versa. Reporting it backwards does not make it valid. Worldwide currencies should be exchanged by valuing them to gold and silver, not to the U.S. dollar, or any other currency for that matter.

It makes no sense to ask whether gold will go to $1,000 per ounce or $10 per ounce, because it is the dollar that is changing its value. Gold and silver change their value very little with respect to goods and services for which they may be bartered. One hundred or two hundred years ago an ounce of gold would buy a good suit of clothes and an ounce of silver would buy a good meal at a restaurant. These metals have not strayed very far from this valuation except under economic tensions, or their dissociation with labor exchange (de-monetization). However, if extreme economic tensions occur in the future, gold and silver will re-associate with our labor bartering and rise in value according to the demand for limited commodities and the demand for metals in exchange for those commodities. The dollar will be irrelevant as a stable standard of labor value, because its supply will be impossible to regulate.

Investment counselors almost universally recommend that all investors should put 10% of their surplus into gold bullion or gold stocks. If there is a general meltdown in the investment markets and our economies, then those who own gold will be able to purchase what will become dwindling goods and services to sustain themselves until new opportunities are developed.

Today, Gold is almost all consumed as investment bullion and jewelry, with a small amount used in industry. Silver is used mostly as an industrial commodity and a small amount is used in making jewelry. So in our current economy the demand for gold as jewelry is much higher than our demand for silver as jewelry, even though silver is more plentiful. Conversely for industrial applications, silver is used much more than gold for good economic reasons. And whereas most gold is used in ways that keep it as pure bullion or make it easily recoverable back to pure gold, silver is to a great extent used in electronics, film, and other industrial products in ways that make it too costly to recover.

As time passes, the ratio of gold available to silver available comes closer to parity. When and if we stop using gold and silver in jewelry and industry, and return to using them as exchange money, we will exchange them according to the amounts that are available to our economies. If there should only be five ounces of silver for each ounce of gold, then silver will be valued at one-fifth the value of gold, not one-fiftieth. In a non-money application these metals are valued correctly by the commodity markets that control their consumption; but in a money relationship, gold and silver and many other valuables will exchange for each other as well as goods and services. When they exchange for each other as money, that exchange will occur according to local economic activity and according to the amount of gold and silver and other scarce valuables available to local economies.

In the past there have been many attempts to peg a monetary ratio between gold and silver. It has been ten-to-one, twenty-to-one and even thirty-four-to-one during the depression. Teddy Roosevelt ran for President promising to fix the ratio at sixteen ounces of silver to one ounce of gold. These ratios not only show a historical variance, they also are all showing ratios of silver to gold that are greater than the real amounts of these metals mined and refined. The reason that these metals are not valued in direct relationship with the amounts mined is principally the hoarding of gold by governments, some international banks, and some international corporations. The hoarding of gold by governments is the same as it having never been mined, as far as the markets are concerned. Investors also hoard some gold and silver, but they are much more likely to make it available for trade or consumption. This hoarding of gold tends to skew the ratio of gold available to consumers and investors as compared to the silver available. And it is a valid factor in arriving at a proper price for gold with respect to silver, provided that this hoarded gold remains unavailable for investment or trade. If this hoarded gold came back into the markets as a monetary unit it would un-skew a gold-silver relationship that goes back to the late 1800's. If governments, however, decide by laws to remove even more gold from private ownership to government ownership, they will do so at their price; and whatever is left in private hands will be too small of a quantity to serve as money. In either case silver would increase in value as compared to gold or any paper currency still around.

Consider that with more than six billion people on earth there simply is not enough gold and silver available to have these precious metals fulfill the role of money for everyone. It is estimated that about 4.4 billion ounces of gold have been mined in historical times and at least 4 billion ounces are still with us as pure bullion, or easily recovered and smelted into pure bullion; this amounts to only two-thirds ounce per person. It is also estimated that about 44 billion ounces of silver have been mined in historical times and about 20 billion ounces of this silver has been consumed in the past and disposed in ways that are not profitable to recover. Approximately 24 billion ounces of silver could be recovered and converted to coins or bullion; this amounts to about four ounces per person. Central banks and governments hold about 800 million ounces of gold and negligible amounts of silver, leaving just over 3 billion ounces of gold and 24 billion ounces of silver in the hands if businesses and individuals; or an approximate ratio of 8 to 1.

If our paper currency fails, causing people to barter with gold and silver for their daily needs and wages, then gold can at most command a value of eight times that of silver. Since the current ratio of value is $750 to $10, or 75 to 1(in the fall of 2008), gold is nearly 10 times higher that it should be relative to silver. This means that silver will appreciate many times over when gold and silver become barter money again. It is less than 50 years since silver was taken out of our US coinage; yet prior to 1964 silver has been in coins going back over 1000 years. While gold has not been barter money since 1934 in the United States, its history as coined money goes back more that 2000 years.

I am not asserting that gold and silver are improperly valued today. But I am asserting that investors who own gold to protect themselves from the calamity of a failed economy and currency are investing in the wrong metal, by a factor of at least eight. Our current use and demand for these metals would have no relationship to the value they would become as barter-money in a failing world-economy. So one cannot compare these metals today and make an investment in holding one of them, based on their current uses and values in our social economy. If a well-to-do person were going to set aside food and other necessities for future consumption in case of economic depression, should they be advised to purchase champagne, caviar, and frozen pastries (gold); or should they perhaps purchase apple juice, sardines, and crackers (silver)? Quantity and quality are more important than show when one is trying to survive, rather than entertain. People who invest in gold as insurance against economic depression are not acting in their own best interest; they are simply following their investment brokers bad advice.

If investors and their counselors really understood the different forms of money, gold and silver, and investing, they would never purchase or recommend the purchase of gold at its current inflated price. Better money, silver, is actually deflated below production costs. If silver is mined at ten ounces for each ounce of gold and is priced correctly at $10.00 per ounce then gold should only be $100.00 per ounce. But if gold is priced correctly at $750.00 per ounce then silver should be $75.00 per ounce. Whichever way the market moves in a panic, silver will appreciate by a larger factor in relationship to gold. Actually, both metals would appreciate with respect to the dollar, but silver would outpace gold in percentage growth at the point where producers and consumers started preferring gold and silver in exchange for goods and services.

In the recent past the U.S. dollar has decreased more than 33% in value against the Euro, German Mark and the British Pound. Other currencies have gone up and some down with respect to the dollar. Gold meanwhile has been very stable with respect to the dollar until 2006, which means all of these other currencies are varying in value, some greatly, with respect to gold. Silver continues to bounce up and down from 11 to 14-plus dollars an ounce. Considering how large our trade deficits are, it has required some remarkable pressure on foreign economies to help keep gold relatively stable to the dollar while they both sink in real value worldwide. The U.S. trade deficit for any recent one-month period is greater than the total U.S. gold reserves. Even though we no longer use gold to payoff such deficits, its existence and amount as reserves are taken into account by all governments and central banks.

The past manipulating of dollar pricing for gold and silver by multiple central banks was not done so much as to cause their prices to appear stable, as it is done to make the "Dollar" appear stable. If the dollar should undergo pressure to de-value with respect to all currencies, volatility in its value would hamper international trade and could even destroy the world economy. While there can be volatility in Iron or Wheat or Cotton with respect to the dollar, due to world consumption demand and fluctuating supplies; for gold and silver, any large moves in price with respect to the dollar demonstrate volatility in the value of the dollar, not in the value of gold and silver. The US dollar is used and preferred by many nations that have no control over its supply. Such faith, if tested, may not hold during international economic crises; at which point the preference for another currency, such as Euros or gold or silver, will force dollars held in foreign reserves to de-value with respect to international debts. If the US dollar is ever dissociated with international trade, its value may take severely inflationary swings, as other nations purge their economies of our dollars and send them back to our shores as payment for goods and services or past debts. What will we do with all of that money in our limited economy?

There is a second action that serves to artificially

manipulate gold and silver prices. Since gold and silver are not used as exchange money, but rather as industrial and investment commodities, investors will not create much activity in these markets if they are always trading at very stable prices. So speculators will not buy into these markets if they cannot produce volatile swings in prices from which to profit. And investors will not hold much gold or silver because holding these metals does not pay any interest or dividends. If investors were to focus on gold and silver they would more readily abandon the dollar, if it devalues. Therefore the Federal Reserve and other central banks are greatly aided in forcing gold and silver to follow the U.S. dollar, by keeping investors and speculators out of these markets. The longevity of coupling gold to the dollar causes more and more investment strategists to assume that gold and silver are very poor investments. As long as supply fulfills demand, and speculation is kept at bay, the metals markets will remain bland and subservient to the dollar. If metals consumption should rise above central bank control, or if speculators decide to call the bluff of the central banks, the price of these metals will soar. The dollar will be very depressed and probably abandoned as an international currency in place of gold and silver or a more stable currency like the Euro, and such pressure could spill over into other resources, devaluing the dollar across the board (rather than devaluing resources as occurred in 1994-95)

In rough economic times gold is almost always used internationally between governments and central banks. Laws can be passed to make citizens sell their gold to governments to pay trade deficits, just as was done in the 1930's. Those who sell, must give up their gold at a price set by government, in exchange for inflating dollars. Silver, on the other hand, is almost always domestic money and is used internally between citizens, banks, retailers, and manufacturers, to carry on business. So an investment in gold may not necessarily allow a person to do anything but sell it to their government, in such a way that they will not benefit as much as they might expect. The value of gold and silver in terms of productive labor and in exchange for goods and services to consume, dictate that silver is much more beneficial to individual and communities than gold. Investors should take note of this when planning for possible future economic duress.

Besides the ratio of gold to silver issue there is another important aspect of gold usage in tough economic times that must be considered; and that is the usage of gold to purchase food, toiletries, medicines, clothes; etc. If we were to do the Zimbabwe thing and have the US dollar inflating 100 % per week while very few goods are available to purchase; anyone going to a store with a shiny 1-oz gold coin would find that their purchases may only use up 10 to 20 percent of the value of their gold coin and that the store cashier would not give them change in gold or silver (even if the store had gold and silver to make change); the cashier would give them change in paper dollars that would rapidly inflate to nothing if they could not be quickly spent. This problem would not occur with silver to any great extent because silver is still available from 100 oz bars down to 1 oz coins, and also available as old US coins, right down to silver dimes, permitting shoppers to pay with exact change for the goods they require. In the late 1970's an elderly Dutch gentleman told me how he experienced this very problem when he was sent to Germany in the early 1920's to go to university. The gold coins he received from home, for living expenses, was greatly sought by the shopkeepers, but they had little to sell and he always received change in German Marks (paper) that lost more than half their value in a week. He seldom got full value for his money, because of daily inflation. The same situation could occur here; it certainly has hit many nations in the last few decades, and for some it lasted many years. Silver is by far a superior investment to gold when it is being held as insurance against inflationary times and economic panics.

Chapter 11 - Standard of Living and Foreign Trade

Social economists often discuss our general welfare and our economic relationships with the term "standard of living"; a gauge of how much goods and services we produce and consume. Historically, except for periods of war, standards of living have improved because of technological innovations and longer production lives of laborers. However, the nations of the world do not sufficiently share technology and therefore they do not have labor forces of equal skill. Standards of living for different nations range from immense wealth to incredible poverty. Similarly within nations, individual societies do not share the profits of technology, so nations also have immense wealth and incredible poverty within their individual borders.

Two principle economic associations determine our standard of living. The first is the amount of our labor we are allowed to keep to exchange with others. The second is the productivity of our labor as compared to all other laborers worldwide. The range of different standards of living throughout the world would start with workers who labor with hand tools and animal power, giving them very limited productivity. While the upper end would have workers who labor with high speed machines, producing thousands of times more productivity than simple hand labor. These extremes are very prevalent throughout the world, with a few rich and many poor nations. In all cases labor is taxed to support government; such that many poor nations are very limited in the services they can offer their citizens, as compared to more affluent nations. Other things being equal, laborers in Central America producing one-twentieth as much as laborers in the U.S. will have a standard of living that consumes one-twentieth of what the U.S. laborer consumes.

The notion of a standard of living is usually applied to distinct political societies such as nations. However, it is important to realize that the world is becoming integrated politically, through the integration of its many economic systems. Our world has a gross international product of goods and services, which are disproportionately owned, disproportionately produced, and disproportionately consumed.

But the different societies are also stratified. The more technically advanced societies force less developed societies to barter and export their natural resources, with little or no labor applied to those resources toward producing finished manufactured goods. At the same time the technically advanced societies do not export raw materials, only finished consumable goods, representing a maximum labor value (wealth) for each product. Whenever raw materials are exported outside their place of origin, jobs, and therefore the labor-wealth of a higher standard of living, are being exported.

The relative standard of living for most countries is established by the oligarchic control of the G-8 nations. Disadvantaged societies are forced to import finished goods for general consumption, even though they have sufficient labor to manufacture for their own needs. They either cannot get raw materials, or they cannot compete in technology to produce consumer goods efficiently. The stronger economies not only control the exports of weaker economies, they control the imports into those economies, and often put up technological and political barriers to protect and maintain these economic disparities; intentionally causing the standard of living in most countries to remain well below that of the G-8 nations.

International trade is a big issue in the industrialized world, especially trade imbalances. Industry and technology have created manufacturing surpluses for local markets and have therefore sought to expand markets all over the world. But because of the imbalance of manufacturing worldwide, and the imbalance of raw resources and energy, there are and have always been trade imbalances. Industrial nations put up barriers called tariffs, which are just import taxes, on imported goods. Tariffs, being in opposition to free trade, protect richer nations from having to compete with the lower production costs of poorer nations. This has the effect of maintaining a great disparity in standards of living of people worldwide. A tariff is a tax on foreign labor paid into our Federal Treasury, which raises the cost of that labor to domestic consumers and thereby makes it less competitive with domestic labor. To some degree, tariffs and trade imbalances interfere with the autonomy of many underdeveloped nations. Foreign governments and corporations may be economically coerced to conduct both internal and external social policies in a manner prescribed by other countries so that they may expand their trade.

The fallacy of tariffs is that they are added costs at the wholesale level, for import goods at a shipping port, such that the government is compensated very little as compared to a final retail price. All brokers, distributors, and retailers add their mark-ups upon the cost of the products, including the tariff. Tariffs should be added in at the point of sale, like a sales tax, allowing a much larger gain for government and less for brokers, distributors, and retailers. This would reduce some of the profit incentive to import, in place of domestic manufacturing.

The overall U.S. standard of living is declining, partially from the increasing amount of unprocessed goods we export. Our decline also comes from the new trend of CO-production of many of our durable goods with foreign companies in foreign lands. The production of many things that we still readily consume has been abandoned outright to foreign companies. The foreign producers and our domestic retailers do not understand that they will not have any consumers in our economy if all of our goods are produced in foreign economies. If too many of our people are unemployed, or working at menial tasks for minimum wage, they will not be able to trade their labor for goods that are manufactured overseas.

Money supply, money circulation, money exchange between countries; all are founded in productive labor and all define and sustain our individual standard of living. The raising and lowering of our standard of living is tied to the economic activity in our community, which is now very much tied to world economic activity. Community isolation no longer exists, but this does not infer that depressed areas of economic activity are a thing of the past. The very nature of modern banking allows banks to move our surplus labor-money to any area of the planet that will provide a profitable return to them, regardless of the effect on our community. Any area that cannot compete with sufficient productive labor, to provide profit for banks and their depositors, will not have investment capital available to build or rebuild. It will therefore cause a decline in opportunities for its workers and an associated decline in their standard of living.

As banks become less provincial and more international, we will tend to develop one economy worldwide, but still have areas in each country that are resource and job deficient. There will not be rich nations and poor nations, but rather rich regions and poor regions within nations. The nation of Haiti, with its multitude of very poor and a small group of wealthy elite, is not an example of where we have come from socially and economically, but rather an example of where most nations are headed.

The increase in the standard of living in one nation or region is often at the expense of reducing or holding down the standard of living in other nations and regions. The long-term benefit of free trade is that it will sufficiently equalize standards of living worldwide to allow us to do away with economic wars of conquest or occupation. The short-term tragedy is that international bankers are deciding where and when change will occur, rather than the people through their governments.

Many in the U.S. would argue that their standard of living has been going up over the last few years, and so it has for some. Overall, it is declining and will continue to decline. It is labor and the apportioning of that labor that establishes a standard of living. Wherever productive labor is being concentrated, a higher standard of living is being established; and wherever productive labor is being reduced, a lower standard of living is being established. These are not sudden events, nor easily reversible. Economies have direction and momentum, established by internal and external forces of ownership and consumption. Even with a consensus of political will to chart a course toward socio-economic security, we must accept that we cannot suddenly jump to the desired path, but we must follow a course wherein we may build towards our desired society without totally or suddenly dismantling our current society. Even where we do not need to retrace our steps, we do have to proceed one step at a time. This requires that we must live as one people, and that we proceed as one people. But alas, we are not and will not be one people.

Our government may not determine each individual's standard of living, but the government does influence the class structure of our economy through taxation of wages and profits. Since there is a finite amount of productivity in a society, some may only have more, when others have less. The diversion of labor from the producing class, via the government to the idle poor, or via the ownership of manufacturing and merchandising to the idle rich, determines the standard of living of the producing class, as well as the standards of living of the rich and poor.

Fires, floods, storms, earthquakes, wars and famines continually remind us that events will occur that can drastically change our individual standard of living. Since our current standard of living is supported by current and past productive labor, any event that destroys or dissociates us from past and present labor will reduce our standard of living.

Since we have historically improved our standard of living by increasing our knowledge and skill at manipulating energy and resources, this should lead us to place education and experience as the most important guarantors of our continued prosperous society. If we fail to store labor in our children, in the form of knowledge and skill, our society will most assuredly decline as we pass on. If we fail to require that all children receive an education and basic social skills, they will fail to contribute productive labor to support themselves and society in general, when called upon to do so.

Legal decisions pertaining to laws of employment and wages also affect our individual standard of living. The courts pursue equality of pay within individual businesses by saying all persons performing a certain set of tasks, at a given skill level, must receive comparable wages. The exception and flaw in these types of laws is that different companies must not discriminate within themselves, but any company can pay more or less for a skill than other companies. The law simply presumes that it should not interfere in the wage negotiations between labor and capital, except in extreme disputes. So where the law discovers discrimination within a company it will be extremely punitive, but it will not even entertain a request to force all industries to pay comparable wages for comparable productivity. The right for an employee to seek higher wages from a different employer is upheld; the right to strike for higher wages is for the most part upheld. So our courts leave it to the competition of the marketplace to force relative pay equivalence outside of the individual corporate structure.

However, the very nature of capitalism is to maintain economic anarchy for profit's sake, forcing pay inequity by forcing wages down, or by reducing labor requirements, by moving a factory overseas and exporting goods back to our economy, without regard to the social consequences. The standard of living of workers bears no importance to the companies that employ them. The courts show a willingness to support an individual's equality in an individual company, while refusing to interfere in an individual's inequality in our overall economy. It is endemic to our socio-economic system that inequality is measured mechanically and minutely on an individual basis by the courts, for each specific case brought before it. The courts prune the tree of inequality one twig at a time, while the roots of inequality remain untouched.

Another player in the structure of world economies is the growing population. Each person is certainly a consumer, and we all desire that they be good producers, producing more over their lifetime than they consume. The world has limited resources, which will cost more in labor to purchase in the future due to competition to consume, and competition for a limited number of jobs producing a limited amount of goods. Jobs will be exported to the lowest-wage bidders, for productivity equivalent to ours. So the standard of living for the First-World laborers has no place to go but down. And in Third-World economies that are currently depressed because resources are being sold as raw materials, standards of living should rise, when they convert those resources to finished goods. In the end, the equivalence of labor will demonstrate that the most any worker can hope to acquire in labor rewards, is the sum total of his or her own labor.

We are selling many of our public and private resources to foreign citizens and corporations, whose surplus labor is exported here to purchase and control our resources, land, and technology. Foreigners are also purchasing some of our debt obligations as investments; this forces us to export more of our gross national product in the form of interest payments on that debt. These activities can only lead to a lowering of American standards of living.

When trade becomes free of tariffs worldwide, and technology for the production of food, clothes, shelter, and transportation is readily available to all nations, we will move rapidly to relatively equal standards of living for everyone. This will not mean that Americans will have to work more and receive less. With technology advancing rapidly, just spreading it around will reduce everyone's workday. Consider that one hundred years ago a workday was twelve hours, six days per week, minimum. About the time of World War One, it dropped to ten hours. During the Great Depression the eight-hour work day and forty-hour workweek was made universal, just to create more jobs. If it were not for all of the debt being created in our government to fund non-workers, and foreign workers through foreign aid, military aid, welfare of the wealthy, World Bank aid, food and medicine aid, etc.; we could go to a 32 hour, or even 24 hour work week, and enjoy the benefits of technology without reducing our present standard of living.

Chapter 12 - Social Security – Trust Fund And Privatization Fraud

The Social Security Trust Fund is a Fraud

In the late 1930's the U.S. Congress established a Social Security Fund to provide for aging and disabled workers, through the Federal Insurance Contributions Act (FICA). This fund is a payroll tax, which in 2005 was just under 7.65% of your wage, and it currently supports both Social Security and Medicare (Social Security is 6.2% and Medicare is 1.45%); employers must also pay just under 7.65% of your wage to match your contribution.

Upon retirement your monthly Social Security check will be calculated relative to your age when you retire and the amount deducted from your wages during your working years. Even though the amount anyone will receive is figured according to their contributions in the past, every Social Security check comes from the weekly and monthly payroll deductions taken from wages and matching money paid by employers in the present. This amount is just over 15% of the gross wages of almost all workers, up to a wage cap of about $88,000 annually (the Medicare portion is deducted to a higher cap). This is a little less than one-sixth of all wage income. If many are working, then one-sixth of that labor may pay higher benefits and take care of the elderly and disabled adequately; if few are working, then benefits will have to be reduced and many of the elderly without other income may live in privation. Obviously the ability for Social Security to pay benefits depends on the ability of our economy to produce income. In essence and in fact 15% of our productive labor is taken to provide the food, clothes, shelter, medicine, etc. that retired citizens need to live on.

By law, any surplus FICA tax collected by the Social Security Administration is transferred to the U.S.

Treasury Department and exchanged for government bonds. The accumulation of these Treasury Bonds is what the government calls our Social Security Trust Fund. This fund, however, is a complete fraud, because the Treasury Department does not invest this money in any manner that preserves it, or require that the government departments receiving it must pay it back in the future. Like all taxes, it is spent as part of the annual Federal Budget and gone forever. It makes no sense to even talk about repayment. Even though these bonds do earn interest annually (additional Treasury Bonds), the interest is a fraud also; these bonds, both principle and interest, do not represent a fund, nor is the administration of this fund a trust, as any dictionary will attest. This bogus fund is just an IOU from Americans to Americans.

In the Reagan, Bush-1 and Clinton years, the Congress and the President attempted to balance the national budget (after the Reagan tax cuts of the early 1980's) by raising FICA taxes beyond what was needed to fund Social Security. The government then took by statute, not borrowed, these excess dollars to help fund our other government expenses: Housing, Education, Defense, etc. But these excess dollars are spent, and the bonds, along with the interest due, are just promises by government to raise the Income Tax in the future when these bonds are due. For the Social Security Administration to hold bonds, redeemable only by the authority of the U.S. Congress to raise the Income Tax to pay off those bonds, and to call those bonds a Trust Fund, is ludicrous and a fraud. The Social Security Administration would have you believe that it will cost taxpayers less to fund Social Security obligations in the future when these bonds are mature and redeemable. It is truly amazing that people this stupid can be given positions of importance and trust in government.

The idea that the Social Security Administration and the Treasury Department are independent entities with legal standing like citizens or corporations is bogus. The Federal government in its entirety has legal standing, but its parts are not similarly independent. The illusion of separation and independence between the SSA and the Treasury is maintained because the FICA tax is a regressive income tax, hitting the working poor harder than the wealthy. The Social Security tax was instituted 25 years after the Income Tax was established by Congress; it would have been simpler in 1938 to raise the Income Tax on everyone to fund Social Security, but then the wealthy would have objected to paying their fair share, so the politicians bowed to the demands of wealth and we are dealing with the continuing misfeasance of our tax structure today. If our society were just now developing a tax structure to pay our collective bills, Social Security would get its funding from the general Income Tax just as The Defense Dept., Education Dept., Health and Human Services, etc.; because we would require that structure to be fair, by being equitable, in how taxes are raised; and fiscally responsible by taxing our productivity to avoid any kind of debt or phony financing scheme.

When the government sells a bond to any citizen, business, or foreign entity, it is obligated to payoff that bond when due, even if that requires reducing other expenditures, including Social Security, or raising taxes; because government must pay its debts first and foremost. We often hear the term "full faith and credit of the government" with regard to guaranteeing the payment of government debt; without which the government could not entice anyone to lend to it. But the "full faith and credit of government" is irrelevant with regard to the Social Security Trust Fund, because when we the people both own and owe a debt, that debt does not exist; and likewise the obligation to pay likewise does not exist; so neither government faith nor credit are applicable in dealing with this issue. It is a mistake for the Treasury Department to issue Treasury Bonds to the Social Security Administration in exchange for surplus Social Security Tax, because it confuses everyone into believing that they are real obligations for payment by the government and the taxpayers that support the government; BUT THEY ARE NOT!

The Social Security Administration has monthly demands on its cash flow, and when its income is projected to be less than its outflow, Congress will need to raise taxes (in one form or another), or reduce benefits to recipients, to keep the Social Security Administration books balanced. It simply does not matter whether Congress raises taxes and that income

149

is given directly to the SSA to meet its obligations, or Congress raises taxes to payoff government bonds held by the SSA, and those proceeds used to fund Social Security. In either case taxes are raised the same amount to cover the cost of maintaining the Social Security system; this was already done once in 1976, before the so-called trust fund was instituted. The Trust Fund bonds themselves are baloney, because they have zero value and liability to we the people.

It should be obvious to all that courts will give trial to cases of debt between different persons, corporations, and countries; but they would not hear a case where a person, corporation, or country was suing itself to collect a debt owed to itself. If the SSA had used its annual surplus to purchase industrial bonds in U.S. companies or government bonds of foreign countries, it would have legal standing to have a court enforce repayment of its investments plus interest, such that the profits of those companies or the taxes of foreign countries could be used by the SSA to support our elderly. Such is not the case with the Social Security Trust Fund. The American people cannot sue the American people to force payment of a debt they owe to themselves. We will either tax ourselves to meet any contemporary needs of Social Security or we will reduce benefits to the level that we can afford. The Social Security Trust Fund would have no bearing whatsoever on how we meet our needs.

Consider a village moron going about his daily life, being given menial tasks by several businesses so that he may have a supporting income. The particular act that determines that this person is a moron is that when he spends his wages he writes himself an IOU for the money spent. If our village moron decided to retire and cash-in his IOU's at some bank; what bank would loan him money wherein he was both the creditor and debtor associated with his IOU's? You simply cannot be in debt to yourself.

Amazingly enough the American people have a government that is operating in this moronic manner. The U.S. Treasury is the part of the moron that spent the money to support us, while handing out IOU's, and the Social Security Administration is the part of the moron that holds some of those IOU's, and thinks they are collateral for which the citizenry may redeem for future income. This part of the moron even accepts additional IOU's as interest on the IOU's that are non-existent spent money. The working citizenry are the bank (taxable income) to which the Treasury and Social Security Administration want to come and cash-in those IOU's in the future.

The United States Government cannot buy its own debt in any form, in any department or agency, and profit by, or receive income from such an action. Government does not invest in corporate stocks and bonds, or own industries to produce profits from goods sold to consumers. It taxes the productivity of commerce and spends those taxes yearly. There is not one penny of money in our so-called Social Security Trust Fund; we may only tax the productivity of the present; and the productivity of the future, when and only when it becomes the present.

The national budget was balanced for the first time in a generation in 1998. In fact, it produced a 70-billion dollar surplus; and 1999, 2000, 2001 had larger surpluses. The surplus dollars sent to the Treasury by the Social security Administration and used by the Treasury to pay our general expenses amounts to another Income Tax; it is in no way an investment that can be redeemed to cover any future need. These budget surpluses are not all from Income Tax; they are mostly from the Social Security Tax, because workers have been overcharged for Social Security for nearly 20 years just to balance Federal Budgets; not to build a trust fund.

It is impossible to protect future Social Security requirements with today's FICA surplus. We can only supply ourselves with more goods and services today, or reduce the taxes to be collected next year, or pay off a tiny portion of the principle on the National Debt. There is no difference in income to government, regardless of its name; Income Tax, Social Security Tax, Medicare Tax, Excise Taxes, Usage Fees for national parks, Import Duties, etc.; all are levied by government to provide income, and spent by government in annual budgets. Government does not tax the past or future and government does not save or invest for the past or future, only the present.

If it truly makes sense to over tax people to support one portion of government and give them an IOU that could be redeemed at a profit in the future, then why not change all of our Income Tax, Capital Gains Tax, etc. into FICA Tax? Such that the Treasury Department could borrow all of our government spending requirements from the Social Security Administration and issue many more bonds from which we would presumably become an unbelievably wealthy country as those bonds mature. We can all turn into morons and live off the interest, without disturbing the principle. Whether the government establishes two types of taxes to fund itself or ten types of taxes is irrelevant; if one or more tax streams take in more than they require, their tax rate is too high; and if one or more tax streams takes in less than it requires, their tax rate is too low. The moving of tax receipts from areas of excess to areas of deficit is internal bookkeeping, not an investment. Excess funds that are spent instead of being refunded are gone and irretrievable.

In our current economy the baby-boomers are moving into their most productive and profitable work years, a relatively large group of taxpayers paying relatively larger amounts of Social Security tax, as well as Income Tax. The current senior citizens are enjoying relative affluence in their standard of living. But a few years from now when the baby-boomers are retiring and swelling the ranks of the non-working, there will necessarily be a higher tax burden to support those retirees. The money that will be available to fund Social Security will depend totally on the ability of future workers to pay taxes to government. And the bonds piling up in the so-called Social Security Trust Fund are void and worthless. If tax income cannot be increased, there is absolutely nothing that government can do to change what is coming except raise the age of retirement and lower the amount of benefits to be paid, to match the amount of tax that can be taken from those who labor in our economy.

We now have the President and some members of Congress proposing to "save" what is not yet in peril (it cannot be broke if it presently produces a surplus). Any truly surplus money will remain quietly in the government's accounts. It will simply be a reserve to defraud the taxpayers of the truth about the full extent of our deficit spending, while the Social Security Administration receives more worthless bonds (IOU's) in their fraudulent electronic trust fund.

Privatizing Social Security

During the political season of 2004, President Bush re-introduced his aristocratic idea of over-hauling Social Security, to allow younger workers the option of directing a portion of their wage income into, as yet undefined, mutual funds invested in the Bond and Stock markets.

Since the FICA Tax collected by the government still exceeds, and will for several more years, the budgeted expenditures of the Social Security Administration; one must ask, what is the real reason for pursuing this course of action regarding wage diversion to the Bond and Stock markets?

Before I answer that question I would like to remind the reader that Congress always has the option of raising the existing tax a small amount; and making all personal income subject to FICA Tax rather than not taxing annual personal income above $125,000; and Congress can also reduce benefits for those that have significant alternative income; and raise the age limit to receive benefits, which has already been done once. All of these revenue refinements are completely un-necessary and non-applicable until the year before the FICA tax withholdings are projected to fall below the projected obligations of the Social Security Administration.

It is wrong to think of Social Security as an entitlement for all who reach a particular age; rather it should be viewed as a safety net for those that are disabled and or economically disparaged, and unable to compete for a job in our economy. We must tax ourselves to take care of those who cannot take care of themselves; and we must bare this burden with a tax that is relative to the income of all workers and the profits of all businesses.

If we consider that the average life expectancy of a working male was 65 years in 1938, when Social Security was being structured by Congress, and it was also the age necessary to begin receiving benefits, we can appreciate why people should be encouraged, if not required, to work longer before retiring. In 1938 you worked until you either died or were no longer competitive in the workplace; today should be no different.

Social Security was meant to be more of a disability income plan than a pension plan. Persons reaching the age of average life expectancy (about 75 years now) are considered to be at a disadvantage physically and mentally as compared to younger people, and therefore should be allowed to retire and still have some income to live on. This assumed disability is obviously a general recognition that we lose abilities with age; and those living longer than 65 years now, should have to demonstrate incapacity or be required to continue working. The workplace is neither as physically nor mentally demanding as it was in decades past, allowing older workers to be productive and profitable to greater ages. It would not be unreasonable to allow workers older than 65 years to receive some Social Security benefits and allow employers to cut their wages by the same amount; to keep older workers employed and their employers competitive. Perhaps just not taking any more FICA tax out of older workers wages would allow them and their employers to maintain their employment at their current "Take-home" wage; this would give their employer a 15.3% break to keep them employed even if their productivity was somewhat less than other workers.

Consider also that the Social Security system has been operating for over sixty years as an inclusive communal fund, where the wages of those presently working are taxed and that money is divided amongst the elderly and disabled, in an ongoing year to year basis, where each retired generation is supported by their children and grandchildren. It has never been an individual retirement fund (IRA) where wages are diverted for the exclusive use of one investor 20, 30, or 40 years down the road. It is not socially cohesive to go from an "all for one and one for all" system, to one that

154

is best described as "every person for himself or herself". Exclusivity cannot replace inclusivity and meet the needs of the aged and disabled; therefore it is impossible for such a maneuver to enhance or save Social Security.

Workers have for many years had access to 401K retirement plans through their employers, as well as Individual Retirement Accounts (IRA's) through any number of financial institutions and brokerages. Younger workers also have lifelong opportunities to invest disposable income in the Bond and Stock markets for their retirement, in addition to the Social Security they will receive. A government sponsored IRA does not offer workers anything new or better than existing opportunities.

So why has President Bush chosen to pursue the diversion of wage dollars into the private Bond and Stock markets? The short answer is twofold; first, to keep the Bond and Stock markets from crashing in a few years, under the weight of Baby-Boomers divesting their IRA's and 401K's to have money to live on; second, to make sure that those cashing in their IRA's and 401-K's make enough money to pay the taxes that will be due to the Federal government; rather than the possibility that if the Boomers loose in these markets, they will lower government income by declaring their losses against any taxes they will owe. IRA and 401K plans associated with the Bond and Stock markets can only produce income for sellers if someone is willing to purchase their stock and bond holdings in those markets; and the demand for money to flow out of those markets must not be greater than the money flowing in, or the equity value of the Bonds and Stocks that retirees are selling will evaporate under supply and demand pressure; causing many of them to go bankrupt, and the Bond and Stock markets to crash, and government income from taxes to be significantly reduced.

The budgeting process of government seems to be misunderstood by almost everyone including the politicians in Washington DC. When government establishes its annual budget, of any given year, it collects taxes weekly, monthly, and quarterly, throughout THAT budget year to meet the expenses of THAT budget; at no time during THAT year, or within

THAT budget, does government perform any services for economic and social situations in the future; government always operates in the present. Taxes may be raised or lowered, and services may be increased or decreased, to accommodate the next annual budget only. Certainly government must project income streams and spending obligations into the future, but that can only be with the intention of balancing income and spending the year before they become the function and priority of government. President Reagan did not raise the FICA Tax in the 1980's to save Social Security into our present time; he did it to raise revenue for immediate spending in each budget of his presidency; which is why we still have a surplus of FICA Tax every year. The current President Bush is attempting to change the tax code regarding Social Security, not to benefit retirees many years down the road as he claims, but to force the diversion of a portion of wages, year by year, into balancing the cash-flow in the Bond and Stock markets. Although it will be a few years before such a diversion will begin to operate; it will operate on a contemporary weekly, monthly, and quarterly basis, just like other government spending; and will have nothing to do with Social Security that would be applicable to its possible problems in the future. It is not possible to know the income-available and spending-requirements of government far into the future; if it were possible, President Bush presumably would not have led us from budget surpluses of 250 Billion dollars a year when he became president, into budget deficits of 450-Billion dollar in just four years; so his vision of Social Security bankruptcy 40 years hence is not visionary.

President Bush, and cohorts, cannot seem to fathom the simple social concept that we produce and provide food, clothes, shelter, medical care, recreational opportunity, etc. in an ongoing basis; and that all levels of government assist in these endeavors by annual budgets derived from annual tax revenues. When government costs go up so must taxes to pay the bills; if taxes cannot be raised, then services must be reduced. There is no valid or beneficial preparation that government can do today that will affect changes in government cash flow years in the future, outside of continually managing the economy to provide jobs for

156

all, with fair taxes from all, and annual budgets that require no public debt whatsoever. Claiming a need to over-haul the Social Security system today for a perceived problem 40-years hence, is a fraud, because it cannot have anything to do with 40-years hence, when taxes would be raised or services curtailed; but it does have everything to do with today and the immediate future.

Any over-haul of Social Security today, will be a forced diversion of taxable wages into the pockets of some special Interest group; and such diversion will not benefit anyone but that special interest group (in this case, other investors in the Bond and Stock markets). Though the President's plan began under the auspices that it would be optional for younger workers to take part in, before that legislation is finalized and passed by Congress it will be mandatory that all younger workers are a part of it, and the amount that must be diverted (Invested?) will also be stated in that legislation.

If the Federal Government deliberately diverts wages into the Bond and Stock markets, and then borrows money to make up the taxes lost from those wages, a sum estimated at 2-Trillion dollars over 20 years, then the very same young people that will be trying to build their individual nest egg, will be saddled with annual interest payments on that two trillion dollars. Their taxes will be raised or services will be cut to pay that additional interest to the debt financiers. Between interest payments on the National Debt, interest payments on future budget deficits, and interest payments on deficits due to tax losses from wages diverted into the Bond and Stock markets, not to mention Income Tax and FICA Tax; the youth of today have little hope of a financial future that will be adequate and secure.

There are no guaranteed prices for stocks and bonds, and therefore no guaranteed income for IRA's and 401K's. Apparently Wall Street has discovered that the millions of Baby-Boomer portfolios that have ballooned the investment markets over the past 25 years are, within a few years, going to be offered for sale to the highest bidder. And like all products sold anywhere, when supply exceeds demand, prices must fall until a sale is made. But Wall Street has a second sword hanging over it, not only must prices remain high so that the Baby-Boomers limit the amount of stocks and bonds being sold, but younger investors will not invest in Bonds and Stocks if prices slump and their own younger IRA's and 401K plans lose value. This would add additional downward pressure on prices that could worsen a crash of the whole Bond and Stock investment systems.

So Wall Street is calculating how much money MUST flow into these markets to satisfy retiring Baby-Boomers and younger investors, and President Bush is ready to accommodate them by diverting wages into kiting the value of certain mutual funds. If the Social Security Administration does not need FICA tax on the funds that will be diverted, then such a program would amount to taxing wages to support those who choose to gamble in the Bond and Stock markets. To be sure, this program cannot have anything to do with saving Social Security; but has everything to do with saving the Bond and Stock markets at public expense. If the Bond and Stock markets should determine that our FICA tax is not large enough to pay for retirees, as well as buying bonds and stocks for younger workers, they will get the politicians to convince you that the amount of wages that can be diverted must be increased to save Social Security further into the future; when they will really only be dipping into your pocket each pay period to divert more of your money into the pocket of a retired Boomer for each contemporary pay period.

It is not possible for everyone to invest in the Bond and Stock market and gain income there from. When the prices of Bonds and Stocks rise faster than income, the increases in those prices represent inflation to future buyers; they will pay more for less, and in general gain less than previous purchasers. If prices do not rise, then those who gain can only do so when others have lost. In the long run, price inflation must be offset with price deflation or that market will bubble and then implode; while brokerage fees and price deflation will negate any former gains for investors as a whole. Over a long term, such a system would be patently unfair for retirees living on a fixed and inflexible income, because during times of economic stress those that must sell to maintain life and limb are transferring

158

their investment wealth to those that not only do not themselves need to sell, but have a surplus to invest at that moment to take advantage of such socially cruel situations.

For the elderly to live in relative security, society needs to promote two situations; first, the elderly should be as debt free as possible, to subsist on limited income; and second, everyone that wants to work should have a job that allows them to support themselves and still pay government a share to help those that cannot work. Nothing else will work, and failure to establish these two situations will result in a social crisis that will not resolve itself peacefully, if it is not resolved fairly.

Chapter 13 - Insurance

Another fallacy of enduring security in our socio-economic system is the concept of insurance. The idea of reducing one's risk of being impoverished by acts of nature, accidents, disease, lawsuits, etc. is certainly both socially and economically sound, to a point. But insurance as protection from life's difficulties is supposed to be seldom if ever used, and the cost should likewise be minimal. However, this is not the current situation. We have become so abusive and unthinking in our manner of building and living in areas subject to nature's undoing, and in our manner of abusing our personal health and well-being, and in our manner of disregarding social honesty and respect for other persons and their property; that we now find the cost of our abuse to be a significant, and for many an un-affordable expense in our lives. We cannot all suffer from a natural disaster and have our misfortune diminished by insurance. We cannot all have major illnesses, whose treatments require our insurance company to pay out more money than we paid into medical insurance funds. We cannot all be rewarded monetarily in lawsuits that are designed to punish acts of ignorance, inattention, intoxication, and bigotry. We cannot bank on insurance to protect our freedom and standard of living.

Insurance cannot make up for the loss or exhaustion of resources. Nor can it cover all of us against unemployment, or catastrophic illness, or old age disability. If we do not save for the goods and services that we will consume when we are unable to work, then we must depend on others to labor for us, using a portion of their labor to pay for our needs. And if over our lifetime we do not contribute as much to society's needs as we expect to consume when we are no longer able to provide for ourselves, then others will ultimately receive less for their labor, since we would have received more for our labor.

Insurance is a lot like a lottery. If a great many people pay a small sum to be in a lottery, then a single winner would receive a great deal of that collective wealth. But the chances of winning would be proportionately small; the gamble being that one-dollar invested would have an extremely small chance of having millions returned. However, if those running the lottery were to draw for a much greater number of winners, say 5% of entrants, which would make the odds such that one in every twenty players would be a winner, then each winner would only receive twenty dollars for each dollar wagered; not nearly the risk and not nearly the return on the investment. Going a little further, if the lottery is to have 50% winners, then the one dollar paid out by the players returns two dollars to the half that won; hardly a lottery. Things are similar in the world of insurance. If we all wager a small sum against the possibility of future calamity, then a great deal of care can be given, if only a few are in need. But if many are in need (if we have many more winners), then we must either contribute much more to pay the costs, or we must expect that very little help will be available. If all of us are to be in need then each of us must be able to carry his or her full share, making the concept of insurance meaningless, and bringing home the reality that those who cannot carry their own burdens will be abandoned to their individual fates. If in the future our stored labor is insufficient, or if society's surplus labor is unavailable, then insurance will become non-existent.

In the field of medical insurance, politics and laws are subservient to economic pressures. There is some socio-economic pressure to provide medical care for workers, and even some pressure to provide medical care for all citizens. Though for those who own the resources and factories there is only a benefit to them in maintaining production of goods or services, to provide the medical care to keep their skilled laborers healthy. If that cost is too high, or if they must contribute to the health and welfare of non-laborers, they will either lobby Congress to change the law to limit their liability, or move their industries to nations that do not require this form of taxation.

It is commendable that many politicians are attempting to divide the available resources more equitably for the sick and disabled. But very little is being done, or can be done, to increase the amount of medical resources that should be available, and likewise very little is being done to reduce the need for these types of resources. The marketplace is at work and profits must be made, even on illness and misery. If the marketplace changes as to how causes and cures are dealt with socially and economically, then we may achieve both equitable division of our resources, and more importantly, a reduction in need for those resources. This would make the concept of insurance a cradle of concern, rather than a sword of despair.

Consider our medical standard of living. We boast about our advances in prolonging life. We expend vast labor-wealth researching ways to combat disease and infirmity. We invest thousands of lives of intellect and technical skill (in the form of doctors, nurses, and researchers) to combat disease. Medicine has become an industry, and the average retired person today is consuming far more surplus labor to pay the medical expense of prolonging their lives, than they contributed to the retired citizens of their working years. But for many working poor in our country the medical standard of living is declining because they do not have any labor-wealth to trade for the exotic and expensive forms of medical treatment being developed. Labor barters for labor, be it medical labor or any other sort.

Medical care depends a great deal on personal wealth and charity, and because of increasing medical technology at ever-increasing cost, medical care will rely more on wealth and charity in the future. Even if we had socialized medicine we would be declining in our medical standard of living. We cannot all have serious prolonged illnesses, nor can we all have organ transplants and other expensive care.

From the perspective of the healthy, the sick are like the economically wealthy. They consume the labor of others, often beyond their ability to ever repay. Consider that research in the 1990's by the insurance industries indicates that 85% of your medical needs will come in the last eighteen months of your life. Whether the patient is one-year-old, ten years old, or one hundred years old, 85% of medical costs are not returning people to a state of health in which they can labor and contribute to the health and welfare of others. That care is only prolonging their lives by an average eighteen months. This may seem as uncaring on my part, but we must understand that there is a limited capacity for medical care, and there is limited capacity for the healthy to pay for that care. Collectively, those who are ill tax the healthy for a portion of their labor to give to the medical industry in trade for medical services. And in a market economy that promotes social classes, the have-nots will get less care, when the haves get more care.

Consider a medical plan for a worker who pays $125 a month for medical insurance. This is $1500 a year. For a working career of 45 years, he or she will pay $67,500 in total. Medical science has discovered numerous treatments and diagnostic tests for many diseases, which will guarantee that this worker could consume far more medical resources than they contributed. If someone receives a $250,000 heart transplant, paid for by insurance, then five of my example workers must contribute all of their lives, but remain healthy and never use any medical insurance, just to pay for this one operation along with the business expenses and profits of the insurance industry. The reward for good health is continuous and ever-increasing medical taxes.

Certainly there is a need for medical care in our lives. But to what extent are we the cause of our medical misfortunes, and to what extent can we expect the surplus labor of others to pay for the burden of our misfortunes? The medical industry is growing and the cost of its growth must come from the surplus labor and productivity of other areas of the economy. We must remember, it is the labor of others that supports the doctors, nurses, researchers, their families, and their myriad facilities, while they go about their lives of fighting ill health for society.

Chapter 14 - National Defense

If peace between nations and diverse cultures resides in their adherence to established treaties and covenants, then a violation of these treaties or covenants in the form of violence against persons and property is the beginning of war. War requires the offensive role of military organizations. And in this role the military seeks to destroy the war making capacities of its country's enemies. The military in action does not defend its own country; so much as it offends any adversary countries.

The inactive role of the military is to serve as deterrence to aggression by other military organizations. Training troops and amassing equipment that would be used to attack an aggressor nation, carries out this deterring role. The greater the military preparedness, the greater the deterrent, and very likely the greater the destruction when military forces are unleashed.

We could broadly define deterrence as a form of national defense. But a precise definition of the concept of defense must exclude deterrence, in order that the concept of national defense could be meaningful. Although we hope our military can thwart any aggression against our nation, we must realize that our military is not empowered to act on its own volition; it is subservient to the civil authority of society.

The laws and customs of a nation comprise its internal treaties and social structure, by which the particular citizens of any nation interact and function as a society. The defense of that society rests solely in the recognition of, and adherence to, the laws and customs established. If citizens, individually or in groups, violate the laws and customs, they are making civil war in their nation. They are promoting anarchy, and if they succeed in de-stabilizing the government, they will have defeated it. Defense of a nation then is an internal matter with the citizens, and is outside the purview of the military, which should be thought as in charge of "National Offense", not defense.

The decay of a society, away from its historic

culture and social cohesion, would tend toward anarchy. In such a situation military organizations cannot attack the perpetrators, nor can it defend the society declining into anarchy. There is no organized enemy in this situation and therefore no way to attack that enemy. A recent example is the decline and decay of communism in Eastern Europe. Both the police and the military organizations were unable to halt the changes going on. They were also to a great degree unwilling to halt these changes. In a society that is only one class of citizens, the police and soldiers are part of that one class, making it difficult for the citizens to be subject to being attacked or defended by the actions of these organizations. In the case where the soldiers and police adhere to and obey the established laws, they also defend the society. When citizens abandon the old laws and customs and establish a new society with new laws and customs, they become the defenders of the new society simply by their adherence to the new laws, not by forming a military or police organization to enforce new laws.

The danger to all societies from without lies in the violation of international treaties and covenants. It is at this time that the military organizations are put to work doing that which their constant training and discipline has made them ready to do - destruction. Destruction by the most violent means, causing the most intense form of anarchy that can befall an opposing society. Acts of war are a far greater example of anarchy being thrust upon societies, than the destruction caused by poorly organized revolutionists, acting violently to serve self-interests. The amassing of troops with their entire ordinance has the one purpose of disrupting social cohesion and destroying stored labor. The irony of war is that it visits the most intense form of anarchy and chaos on a society, by using the most structured and disciplined efforts of the opposing society, acting with a single purpose. It is not simply the destruction of property and the death of soldiers that makes war a tragedy. It is that soldiers are a very valuable resource as civilians, with knowledge to build and preserve their respective societies, with strength to transform the resources of the Earth into products that lighten the burdens of life.

166

War is an extension of economic activity. It is used to take land and resources where they cannot be reasonably purchased. It is used to destroy competitive economies that could not be destroyed in the marketplace. The economic structure of resource ownership and labor availability forces societies to develop both a supportive internal economy, and an external economy of surplus labor and surplus resources, to promote international trade. For hundreds of years, different societies have risen in economic power pursuing a disparity of ownership in their favor, and resorting to weapons of destruction to protect and promote their society at the expense of other societies. Economic warfare has been going on for thousands of years, and untold millions of soldiers and civilians have been sacrificed on this bloodiest of altars; the control of labor, land and resources.

When the Germans and Japanese could not take, through wars of conquest, the resources and foreign labor to feed and support their economies, they had to turn to their own labor and a generation of sacrifice to build and compete for market-share and self-sufficiency. They appear to have finally achieved the goals that they had in the 20th century. They now have access to resources from many lands, and they profit from the control of labor in many nations, by forcing others to support the social pyramid that international economic warfare always seek to build. But no society has dominated other societies for very long without resorting to outright marshal law, military aggression and war.

This planet will not know peace until its diverse cultures can adopt and maintain between them the same social discipline that they all seek to establish and maintain internally. Forcing diverse cultures to recognize an external authority, such as a worldwide central government, will not allow peace to prosper. Allowing diverse cultures to war upon each other for religious reasons, failing to recognize that we all exist by the will and authority of the Creator will not allow peace to exist. Failure by diverse cultures to join in international consensus building regarding the uses and availability of the Earth's resources will only maintain the perceived need for military deterrence. This will not only prevent peace from being established, but will always hasten war, as we have seen for hundreds of years. If we do not recognize that we only have freedoms when all others have them, that we only have security if we guarantee security to all others, then someday we will experience anarchy in all its forms, in all our undertakings.

War creates hatreds and enmities that can last generations. It uses up the Earth's resources at a tremendous rate. Yet we are far more disposed to act with a single purpose, to sacrifice without concern for the cost, when we have it in mind to destroy the culture and property and future of others.

Like insurance, our national defense system reduces our standard of living. It consumes labor and resources contributed by the rest of society as taxes, to cure the supposed disease of international social disharmony. In many cases the military are little more than mercenaries, employed by a political-economic aristocracy. They consume the milk and honey of their society, while offering services of protection to the owners of the resources, land and labor. The owners of the defense industry profit from the manufacture and use of weapons that are built, paid for, and operated with working class labor. The working person's standard of living is not increased when we go about the destruction of another nation's social infrastructure and industries. The defense industries do contribute taxes to the many levels of government. They do contribute to the health of all areas of our economy, but we must learn to measure their existence as a sacrifice by the rest of us. Their contributions to the economy are but a small refund on an enormous expense. I do not wish to appear to insult the history of our military and what many perceive as a noble sacrifice, but I do want to make plain the cost of perceived threats to our common security.

The entire military establishment, and all of the industries that support it, cost approximately 450 billion dollars per year (2004). If we were to divert that effort to digging large holes in some desert and filling them in again, over and over, consuming energy and machinery and material, we would have accomplished as much for the economy as our current national defense structure does now. The cost to the rest of society would be the same. Four hundred and fifty billion dollars spent anywhere in the economy will roll over several times, having numerous opportunities to be taxed to help defray the expense of all levels of government. Those 450 billion dollars are an expense and a sacrifice by the rest of the country, to provide work for the military and the defense industries. The producing class in other areas of the economy must generate those 450 billion dollars from their surplus labor.

If the hole diggers and fillers had turned their labor to manufacturing and transporting durable goods, we would have more goods available to more people at lower costs, reducing tax burdens and reducing the amount of labor we all need to contribute to our own sustenance and future welfare. We got the Russians to convert many of their defense industries into manufacturers of durable goods (TV's, refrigerators, washers & dryers, trucks & autos, etc.) for their own consumption. In this country we talk about the hardships that will occur for our defense laborers and military personnel if we cut back.

It is a mistake to believe that we must keep building weapons which can only annihilate all societies worldwide, to avoid massive unemployment in the defense industries. These people have been unemployed, for all intents and purposes, for all time. It would not cost our economy any more to lay them off from their jobs with full pay and benefits. We could even save money by not paying the enormous profits demanded by the owners of the resources that are consumed in building all of those weapons. And those newly unemployed defense workers, who are conscientious and patriotic, could go out and offer their services to government, community and industry, at no charge, since they would be paid from the defense budget. The rest of society would benefit from their labor by being able to produce more goods for trade or consumption, or by reducing the hours that we need to labor to produce the goods we currently consume, or a little of both.

Conservatives complain about welfare, Medicaid, and other social programs as being un-capitalistic and leading to socialism, while they harangue for a larger and larger defense establishment. There is no larger group of socialized citizens than our military personnel, civilian government employees overseeing defense, defense contractors and their families, and the communities that rely on their paychecks. All of them are feeding from socialized weapons manufacture, distribution, and use, which are paid for by other middle class taxpayers. There is no real competition in the defense industries. There is however, abundant corruption and greed. The difference between social welfare socialism and defense socialism is the profit potential for the defense industries to profit from the forced contributions of taxpayers.

We all consume goods and services, and there is a limited amount of production of goods and services worldwide at any given time. Those who are employed in digging and filling holes, or employed in militaries and defense industries, or who are poor and unemployed, or who are unskilled and unemployable, or who are skilled but unemployed, or who are physically ill, mentally ill, or aged and unable to work, are all drawing their sustenance from the productive labor of others. This is not to say that all of these people do not deserve what they receive, the abundance of the Earth, and our capacity to labor, are more than sufficient to carry those truly in need. Great amounts of food, clothes, and shelter are available when great amounts of labor are applied to the natural resources of the Earth. Society provides and promotes these labors. It must be able to support those who are unable to provide their own labor. But the military and the defense industries should not unnecessarily feed off society as if they were welfare cases. Their contribution to our general welfare in the form of goods and services could be more profitable for our society, if those dollars and that productive capacity could be put to better use creating items for general consumption, and the relief of pain and misery.

Chapter 15 - Rights

Rights, rights and more rights. Rights for some, rights for all, denied rights, new rights, old rights, universal rights, equal rights. You would think that with all the public chatter about rights we would have a better understanding of rights; what they are and what they are not, and exactly where they come from.

In fact, there are no such things as rights. The common notion that we are born with some universal baggage, called rights, is nonsense. There is no right to life, liberty, or the pursuit of happiness. From wars and disease and famine, to accidents and crimes, to abortion, to self-destruction by any number of means, people die against their wills by the thousands every day. The liberty and happiness we all hope to enjoy is as much an exception as most believe it to be the rule. The current destruction of life, liberty, and happiness, worldwide, should be enough to convince anyone of the fallacy of our current concept of rights.

Much of our social interaction is founded on tolerance; specifically the tolerance or intolerance of each other's behavior. Tolerance, when it is universally taught and accepted, is called a right, and for many it has its own separate existence apart from social structure. Tolerance is not separate from any social structure. In fact, our limits of or refusal to limit behavior define our social structure. Tolerance belongs to the community or the state, not to the individual, and therefore there are no such things as individual rights. While community rights (tolerance) change with every new law.

So rights as they are described in today's societies are really just the types of behavior that are to be tolerated by all. Any behavior that interferes with the tolerable behavior of others is itself not to be tolerated (not a right). One fundamental purpose for constituting governments is to establish and enforce rules of social and economic behavior, since we come into the world without rights to protect us from the possible abuse of others.

The fundamental principle of government, from our primitive civilizations to that of Galactic governments is found in all cultures and all histories, and simply stated is, "Do unto others as you would have them do unto you." No person can be free who does not live by this principle. No society can enjoy domestic tranquility if any of its citizens fail to adhere to this principle. No government can endure that does not enforce this principle. We are obligated to obey and uphold this fundamental principle at all times. It should not be the focus of our social interactions to say that we have individual rights. It is more important that we recognize our social obligation to support society's rules and communal liberty over any individual liberty.

Some members of every society do not live by this principle, and are given to interfering with the tolerable behavior of others, so some restrictions on social behavior must be established and enforced.

The inversion of the above fundamental principle is the foundation of past social revenge; "An eye for an eye, a life for a life . . ." To deny another person of liberty, means you accept that you may have your liberty denied. To deny another person of life means you accept that you may be denied life. Any act that a person may commit that transgresses the accepted laws of behavior denies that person protection from societal revenge.

It is common in our society to hear reference made to the work of the courts as dispensing justice. Whenever we agree with the ruling of a court, we say justice has been done. But the courts cannot dispense justice, because justice is not something that can be dispensed. Justice can be done, but not by the courts. Justice exists in a society only when the laws are obeyed, because we do justice to each other when we obey the laws.

When the laws are obeyed domestic tranquility is established in society. Justice and Domestic Tranquility are really the same concept, adherence to established law. To understand one, is to understand the other, because each is a definition of the other.

The inverse of justice is injustice. When someone transgresses the laws, thereby destroying the domestic tranquility, we say an injustice has been done. All transgressions of the law can be generalized as a breach of the peace. This is not said to equalize or

172

trivialize all crime, but instead to point to the collective relationship of all our acts toward each other, as being acts that affirm domestic tranquility, or acts which breach the peace. With our multitude of laws there are no real gray areas of social behavior. Our actions both defend the community structure and maintain the domestic tranquility, or they violate the established law by attacking the community, trying to usurp its powers and defeat its social order.

So where do the courts come in? If no laws are transgressed, then no police or courts are necessary. However, since laws are often broken, we have contrived a system whereby we take collective social revenge upon the persons who commit these injustices. We do this through our police, courts, and prisons. Courts cannot dispense justice, but they can dispense revenge in one manner or another by restricting or denying the freedom to live and work in society. If this revenge or punishment is dispensed in such a manner that society is guaranteed that no further transgressions will be committed, then we may say that society has been returned to a state of domestic tranquility. However, if the courts fail to ensure the proper behavior of those brought before them; if there is little or no revenge sought against those that destroy the domestic tranquility; if there is no guaranteed rehabilitation; then the courts are aiding and abetting future crimes, committing an injustice of their own by preventing society from re-establishing domestic tranquility. Such failure in the courts will lead society away from the fundamental principle of government into a state of anarchy. If we fail to revenge ourselves as a society, we will do it individually. This would be anarchy, and would destroy our social structure.

After the alarm has sounded in the community that a crime has been committed, what are we told to think? "Innocent until proven guilty." Our social-judicial system does not operate under the principle "innocent until proven guilty." In the area of civil law where many frivolous suits are filed, and where degrees of liability are difficult to estimate without legal expertise, we may accept that the defendant is innocent until proven liable; but in criminal law we hire or elect legal expertise in the form of prosecutors to investigate, charge, and prosecute those whom they have sufficient evidence to charge with criminal behavior. The prosecutors are our representatives in the legal system. If they bring charges against someone, it is because they believe that person to be guilty beyond a reasonable doubt. We hire these experts to formulate knowledge of criminal activity, based on factual evidence. If we are to believe the accused to be innocent, then we must believe that our court representatives are either corrupt or incompetent in pursuing the prosecution of innocent people. Though there are instances when officials are corrupt or incompetent, and instances when innocent people are put in prison or worse, these circumstances occur very seldom as compared to the great number of prosecutions ongoing. If the vast majority of criminal prosecutions end in conviction of the accused as being guilty as charged, then the idea that a person should be considered innocent (not guilty) after they have been charged, is ridiculous.

Common sense demands that we support, intellectually and socially, those whom we have hired to represent and enforce our social structure. Criminals and their counselors are defeating our society as a system of law and order. When criminals violate the liberty and property of others, they are making war upon society, trying to defeat the law and order that bind societies. They are much more the enemy of society than foreign armies.

When we are charged with a felony crime against other persons or property, the court requires that we post bail to gain temporary freedom; we are guilty in the eyes of the court even if no other bias is ever shown. At trial, evidence is then presented to the court and a jury, which will then proclaim to society our guilt or innocence. In many cases bail is denied because a judge not only perceives considerable evidence toward guilt, but may also consider the defendant likely to flee from the community to avoid the consequences of being found guilty by a jury. Certainly guilt must be proven beyond a reasonable doubt, and should never be assumed, especially if no charges are brought against persons except community gossip, hearsay, and fabrication. But when charges are brought, evidence is presented, and indictments handed down from a court,

174

innocence must likewise be proven, if it is truly the case.

Actions in court are not supposed to be a competition of diverging beliefs communicated to the public for the purpose of establishing majority opinion. But rather a merging of testimony and facts, to arrive at the truth that society requires to re-establish domestic tranquility. A mature way to view these concepts in relation to a person charged with a crime is to realize that neither guilt nor innocence applies to a defendant that has been duly charged, until a jury has made a determination.

We sometimes fail to understand that tolerance, which we claim as necessary for ourselves may also be claimed by others, but for their own selfish ends. And that tolerance we would deny others may also be denied to ourselves, with or without due process. There is no law of self-preservation that is part of any social structure, as some would have us believe. The sacrifices made daily to save other persons and property at the peril of life and limb; the many instances of heroic bravery in wars; the lifelong sacrifices of one's comfort and leisure, so that one's children will be better fed, clothed and educated; are proof that we recognize sacrifice to be more noble than self interest. The coward runs from battle to preserve himself. The criminal preys on society for property and money, so that he may preserve himself. The profligate abandons morality and social responsibility to serve himself. Self-preservation only succeeds in destroying social structures. Anarchy knows no peace and guarantees no trust. The tolerance we require, we must also offer; and the social discipline we expect of others, we must also be willing to uphold.

To demonstrate that self is becoming the root cause of our social declension, consider the story from olden times about a survivor of the judgment of Sodom and Gomorra. As the story goes, this survivor was discovered by a caravan, living near the ruins of Sodom. Surveying the destruction all about them, the leader of the caravan exclaimed to the survivor that he must have truly feared the Law of God to have been spared. The survivor replied, "I was not spared because I feared the Law of God, I was spared because I loved the Law of God and I obeyed the Law because of that love and what it means; those who obey the Law are free from the Law." The selves of today are more and more disposed to abandon the principle of community and the preservation of family and society above the preservation of self. The transgressors of the law fear the laws, because they fear society taking social revenge against them, preventing them from doing their particular forms of anarchy and oppression. An important fact of most criminal behavior is that criminals have consciously chosen before hand to abandon their social obligations to support and protect society, and instead have chosen to prey on society without regard to the often-tragic consequences. And yet the increasing numbers of these transgressors, who continually use the current court system to evade accountability, is burying us. They offer excuses for inexcusable behavior, citing their demand to be treated and forgiven according to an established body of law, which they would gladly have destroyed, were it in their power to do so. They exhaust our resources and our access to the courts to deal with less serious transgressions. The criminal justice system is forced to barter with the flood of criminals, in hopes of redirecting behavior by threat rather than by restriction and education.

The majority of citizens have grown up in a society that offers them education and opportunity to labor and contribute to the needs of others. Currently less than half of our population is employed in productive labor, yet we enjoy an abundance of goods and services. We have constructed a penal system that maintains hundreds of thousands of people incarcerated at a very large expense to our society. These people are not put to productive and rehabilitative labor to ensure that they are not a continuing burden on society. They are not coerced to expand their education and skills, to be truly rehabilitated. A population of relatively young men and women, without financial obligations to themselves, their families or victims, should be put to work supporting the prison systems that must maintain their separation from society, until they learn to uphold and promote the community. Rather than being a burden to society, prisons should be fully self-supporting and able to offer help to the victims of crime.

Rights are not things, but instead are the fundamental behaviors that consensus tells us should be tolerated by all members of society. This leaves very little room for selfishness and no room for oppression. The fallacy of civilization is that it has declined from Ten Commandments, into legal libraries containing hundreds if not thousands of books on law (behavior); rather than inclining toward the Fundamental Principle of Government, "Do unto others as you would have them do unto you!"

There are acceptable behaviors and unacceptable behaviors, which must be learned and passed on to each generation. Failure to learn will result in failure to teach, which will result in failure of social cohesion. The use of the word "rights" will most certainly continue in reference to our behavior; but the personalizing and directing toward self will only continue to confuse our interactions. As individuals we expect toleration of our actions, but that toleration comes from the community, or state, or world, and therefore belongs to the structure of the community, or state, or world. It does not belong to the individual.

Chapter 16 - Treaties

Treaties are the foundation for all of our social interactions. The complexity of bureaucracies creates a distance of government from the citizenry, which often masks the simple treaty principles that are at work in our social relationships. In applying the fundamental principle of government, "Do unto others as you would have them do unto you", we come up against the social distinctions that define the many and varied cultures throughout the world. These distinctions have more to do with required behaviors and taboo behaviors, than with the anarchic lust for complete freedom, currently in vogue in many Western societies. In societies as small as the tribe, clan, or congregation, the first lessons in primary government are to learn what the proper social behaviors should be. Living in proximity to other cultures also requires that societies develop treaties to provide guidelines for interactions between different cultures.

We often think of treaties in connection with our relationship with Native Americans, and with disarmament pacts with the former Soviet Union. Actually, all of our political documents are treaties, and all of our political actions are an affirmation of the treaties in place, or a request that they be altered or abolished. Our treaties begin with our individual social relationships, and progress up to community, state, national, and international relationships.

The original thirteen colonies of America entered into a confederation to fight the British. Since they each considered themselves to be independent states, this confederation was really a treaty establishing the mutual recognition of independence and a responsibility to cooperate with the other colonies. The actions and interactions of citizens as groups, which settled the whole country, have been a day-to-day history of negotiation, except in the destruction of the native population; consensus, except for exclusion of minorities; elections; affirmation of the dominant culture; and continual change.

The success of this system has been the ability to make changes - rewrite our treaties - at all levels of society, and to guarantee basic liberties by holding citizens and their representatives both responsible and accountable for their actions. Accountability has been a key to this system, since no treaty is of any value if the parties to it are not accountable to answer for any and all violations of its terms. Should corruption of trust and authority become entrenched in our system of government, wherein we fail to hold accountable those who violated a trust, or exceeded their authority, or breached the peace and domestic tranquility, we will have abandoned the treaty form of government and set ourselves on a path to anarchy and revolution.

Morality is the voluntary discipline of citizens to obey the laws in public and private; and a moral code is the entire set of laws through which each citizen's assent establishes and maintains such discipline. It may be very lax and limited, or all encompassing and strict. Today we contrive a social morality that is a culmination of today's social laws mixed with religious customs handed down from our ancestors. We have by treaty separated religion and government in our society because of a history of religious persecution, and because there was no one religious group in 1776 that would be a majority voice above all others. We allow communities to operate on a religious power structure, provided they adhere to a national policy of tolerance dictated by the Constitution. But it is a defect of social order to separate government and religion, or at least a defect of religion if we are required to separate social government from religious government. If government establishes a minimal amount of social discipline within our conglomerate society, and various religious groups establish other levels of social discipline for their followers, then these religious groups are required to accept behavior by other citizens, in their neighborhoods, that they hold as intolerable by their members. This separation of church and state forces the strict to submit to the libertine. It requires morality and restriction to be discarded in place of profligacy.

The purpose of religion is to provide a code of behavior, such that social harmony can exist when all citizens choose to adhere to that code. This, coupled with a belief system about the Universe and knowledge of our contemporary environment, will allow citizens to enjoy the most liberty and security, without sacrificing one to achieve the other. Government separate from religion provides a very generic code of behavior centered on the liberties of the individual. As the social order provided by religions disappears, laws are multiplied again and again to expand the general definition of what is permissible and what is not. When religion completely disappears the social order will be a very large and sterile compilation of laws and regulations to promote social mediocrity.

If you combine an ever-increasing legal code with burgeoning greed and corporate self-interest in the control of jobs and the economy, then society will disintegrate under the weight of socio-economic conflicts. Such conflicts would not exist if government were in part a belief system that could create a correspondence between sacrifice and commitment and the desired goals of security and prosperity. Such a system requires recognition of equality of opportunity, of capacity, and of accountability associated with obligations. This cannot be established simply by enforcing a social code of laws, but must be taught and accepted in schools and homes. Societies can be protected from internal chaos by making their moral code a shield, or by making it a sword to wield to protect society from those who choose to violate the moral code in place. Our society is changing from one that in the past relied on school, home, and church to provide a shield of commitment and voluntary sharing to protect the community. Today we are dismantling the shield and creating swords to convict those who violate the social laws. The swords will not be sufficient to save us from decay and revolution. Moral codes, social codes, and treaties cannot continually be multiplied, or subdivided, or expanded, without the loss of liberty. To the contrary, if a society is growing in knowledge, capacity, and commitment it must reduce its code of laws to being fundamental principles only, so that it may provide greater liberty to those who have demonstrated that they will not abuse it.

A generic code of social behavior does not teach its citizens to expect future rewards, or retribution, or to comport themselves daily to promote harmony today and always. A generic code attempts to establish the bounds of liberty of the individual, causing each citizen to view himself, or herself, as an island of wants and needs. Such a code of laws is barely a universal treaty because the delay and difficulty of dealing with transgressions causes the code to be only partially enforced. Eventually the parts that cannot be enforced will be abandoned. Decay continues, anarchy will rule, and the strongest and cruelest individuals will abuse the weaker.

This is a matter of choice. One can choose to be a part of a community, to sacrifice with and for others, to provide liberty and security from want for the whole group. Or one can choose a course of individual effort, matching strength and skill with others, accepting the fate of conquering or being conquered by others. Ultimately the individualist loses liberty, both because others are stronger and force us to serve them, or because he has ruled over others in the past, making servants of them, and he must pay back the servitude he took by force. Since our ultimate growth will be towards sacrifice and cooperation, refusing to own or be owned, the only progressive social code of laws is one that promotes community liberty and sovereignty.

Politicians are paid to construct laws and regulations in response to the will of the people. However, our ancestors have given us a legal foundation that prevents, or at least makes very difficult, the changing of this legal foundation. We are more disposed to accept the rule of law from a time when none of us were yet alive. It is our civilization that is transforming, not our forefathers'. We are responsible for all progress and all problems and all decay in our communities, states, and nations. If our treaties are failing to protect and provide for us, then we must alter them to provide for our future security and happiness. If our treaties do not offer equal protection and opportunity to all of the world's citizens, we will continually be left to engage in wars to reapportion the Earth's resources.

One concept of civilization that appears to fog if not confuse our social thinking is the notion that civilization is ancient. In reality, civilization is only as old as those who actively teach what they have learned. The civilization of today is a mixture of the culture,

182

morals, and the technical skills available to construct and or provide for the social economy. Civilization is the present, so it must operate in the present. The constitutions and laws should be re-affirmed, altered, or abolished actively, not passively. The dead should not rule the living.

Almost daily we alter our society by increases in our knowledge of our planet and life on it. Through locating new resources and new ways of growing food, constructing buildings, transporting goods, handling information, curing disease, etc.; we adopt new ideas and methods into our culture, and abandon old ones. The product of our ways and means is our culture. Our civilization is always modern, even if we function in ways and have customs that are hundreds of years old. We do not get our culture from the past, we get it from the present, from our parents and peers, who got it from their parents and peers, and we produce or modify other parts of it. Civilization is the present. It is manufactured and modified every day. And because our civilization is modern, because it is us, though it may lack civility or even be in decay, it should reflect our thoughts and desires, not those who have long since past on.

We pay people to sit on the highest court in the land with a primary purpose of attempting to discover and interpret the philosophy of past lawmakers, and to pass judgment on our current social conflicts based on these interpretations. If we need to alter the social treaties between ourselves, we must not do so by seeking to determine how other people would have developed law to solve future problems unknown to them. When the Supreme Court finds an action by Congress or some state or municipality to be in conflict with the Constitution, it should not rule the new law to be unconstitutional. It should instead notify the citizenry of the nature and substance of the conflict. The citizenry should modify the new law if that would benefit them, or change the Constitution, so that the law of the land reflects and establishes the treaties by which they are willing to live.

The longevity of a social structure is tied to both the manner of ownership of natural resources and the manner of ownership of our past labors, stored in buildings, factories, energy plants, etc. If the populace is sufficiently fed, sheltered, and protected in their persons and property, they will support any system that sustains that security. But if those of wealth and power only seek to secure their own protection from want, and protection of only their own persons and property, then society is headed for major change.

The signs of change are easy to spot. Whenever people seek changes in the social treaties, they are usually confronted by those who will not profit in, or may in fact lose wealth and future opportunities for wealth, when changes do occur. This confrontation may be legal action in the courts, political action in the legislatures, or police actions in the streets. Court actions are fairly benign because they concern established law. Anyone not satisfied with a court decision can pursue the creation of new laws through their legislature. The political process, more often than the courts, can be corrupted by economic influence, preventing many desired social changes from happening. The remedy for this situation is usually the ballot box. If the election process is corrupted, then those who seek change will resort to direct actions in the streets.

Although cities and counties have very small police forces in relation to their populations, our social discipline and structure make it fairly easy for the police to maintain that social structure, corrupt or otherwise. But when the police are called out to quell civil disobedience, or further, to seek help from the National Guard and or the Army, to keep the social structure functioning, that society has only revolution in its future. There is enough social history extant to demonstrate that those who have the wealth and political power are always undone when they seek to preserve or expand their wealth and power at the expense and or destruction of the lower classes.

Courts, legislatures, and armies of revolution, are our only recourse to apportioning economic and political power. The abuse of the first two is remedied by the third. Societies have been using all three of these arenas of change for thousands of years. When we establish the principle "do unto others, as you would have them do unto you," as our fundamental principle of government, we will be able to dispense with revolutions altogether, and courts and legislatures will be seldom needed. Society will be community based, fraternally structured, and spiritually led; and the treaties by which they control their actions will be unanimously desired and supported by all members.

Chapter 17 - Constitution vs. Declaration

In exploring the workings of governments; the bureaucracies that define how they interact with the citizenry, and how the citizenry are manipulated for political and economic purposes; I have learned that there is a great deal of confusion in the average citizen concerning the formation of governments and the power available to preserve those governments.

A good example is the lack of understanding of our own historical foundations. Europeans discovered the Americas and associated islands over 250 years before some of the British colonies seceded from the British Empire, and established their own governments. For over two and one half centuries the laws of Britain along with the colonial laws, approved by Britain, provided to the citizenry their social, economic, and political structure. With the increasing development of the colonial economies and the abundance of resources for manufactures and trade, England continually taxed the Colonies of their productive labor and resource wealth. Economic disparity with England, reinforced by the social and political disparities between England and the Colonies, was the motivation for colonial self-determination and desire for complete control and ownership of the wealth generated by the Colonies.

Thus was born the Declaration of Independence; a very strange document, whose validity cannot be argued in any court, since it predates any court that its formulators would recognize as a valid court. The authority claimed by those who wrote this document is placed by them above all other. However, the U.S. Declaration of Independence and the U.S. Constitution with its Bill of Rights, are in such great conflict with each other, that they mutually exclude the authority of the other to be the vehicle by which society may establish, promote and preserve its government; to enforce the authority of one is to negate the authority of the other. It is impossible to believe that both of these documents are valid in their exclusive philosophies.

From the Declaration of Independence:

"When in the Course of human events, it becomes necessary for one people to dissolve the political bands which have connected them with another, and to assume among the powers of the earth, the separate and equal station to which the Laws of Nature and of Nature's God entitle them,...} {...That they are endowed by their Creator with certain unalienable Rights, that among these are Life, Liberty, and the pursuit of Happiness. That to secure these rights, Governments are instituted among Men, deriving their just powers from the consent of the governed. That whenever any Form of Government becomes destructive of these ends, it is the Right of the people to alter or to abolish it, and to institute new Government, laying its foundation on such principles and organizing its powers in such form, as to them shall seem most likely to effect their Safety and Happiness. Prudence, indeed, will dictate that Governments long established should not be changed for light and transient causes; and accordingly all experience hath shown, that mankind are more disposed to suffer, while evils are sufferable, than to right themselves by abolishing the forms to which they are accustomed. But when a long train of abuses and usurpations, pursuing invariably the same Object evinces a design to reduce them under absolute Despotism, it is their right, it is their duty, to throw off such government, and to provide new Guards for their future security.}.....{ We, therefore, the Representatives of the United States of America, in General Congress, Assembled, appealing to the Supreme Judge of the world for the rectitude of our intentions do, in the Name, and by authority of the good People of these Colonies, solemnly publish and declare, That these United Colonies are, and of Right ought to be, Free and Independent States; that they are Absolved from all Allegiance to the British Crown, and that all political connection between them and the state of Great Britain, is and ought to be totally dissolved; and that as Free and Independent States, they have full Power to levy War, conclude Peace, contract Alliances, establish

Commerce, and do all other Acts and Things which Independent States may of right do. And for the support of this Declaration, with a firm reliance on the protection of divine Providence, we mutually pledge to each other our Lives, our Fortunes and our sacred Honor."

This sounds like pretty strong stuff. Why would the Colonies, which were being treated like Third World countries, want to justify their intentions and subsequent actions? Principally because the validity of any government formed to control the myriad duties of government, must follow from some authority. When the British, and other peoples, were colonizing the world, they governed by the authority of their King or queen and their Parliament. They enforced their authority with their army and navy. The American colonists needed some equal or greater authority to justify their illegal insurrection, and proceeded to claim that authority from the Creator. The Declaration informs us that the elected representatives of some of the colonists had received authority from some of their constituents to dump the British government and to form an independent government for each Colony. Since you had to be white, male, and a property owner, just to be a constituent, it is unlikely that any natural law or divine authority could be forthcoming from such a limited group.

The authors of the Declaration have informed us that the "Laws of Nature and Nature's God" entitle self-determination; that people are endowed by their Creator with certain unalienable rights; and that these authors appealed to the Supreme Judge of the world to claim validity for their actions; and that they prayed for the protection of divine Providence for their undertakings. These authors were in fact claiming divine authority for their intentions. The common citizen of the time had no authority to give. Over two hundred years later it is still not clear if this authority from the Creator is a one shot deal, or if any group of people willing to exercise self-determination may also use this exquisite authority.

Oddly enough, the United States Supreme Court could not rule on the legality of anyone forming a government in a similar manner. To rule in favor of such an action would be to interfere with a foreign power. To rule against such an action would be to negate its own existence, and thereby render all of its decisions null and void. The Supreme Court is limited to only verifying whether or not a legal argument brought before it is constitutional within the framework of the United States Constitution. No constitution has the authority to void or nullify the formation of other constitutions. The Supreme Court cannot rule on the validity of the United States Constitution itself, and is thereby unable to legally rule on the validity of any other constitutions. The legality of insurrections and revolutions must always be determined by a different court than we can peacefully convene on Earth; namely, the court of war.

After gaining the necessary authority to justify their actions, the colonists then proceeded to raise an Army and a Navy, which after a long and difficult war, were able to demonstrate to the British Army and Navy that they no longer had any power to enforce British political and economic authority in the American Colonies.

So what did these free, independent, and self-determining Colonies do to further this God-given opportunity for any peoples to claim the right of self-determination? They formed a Confederation, elected a Congress that could appoint military men, and gave to them the necessary authority to unite the Colonial Armies and Navies into one force. After the war they formed a new Continental Congress, which established a Constitution founded on the authority of the confederated congress and its Army and Navy. They proceeded to enact statutes that forbade divine right as a justification for establishing government, as being invalid and illegal. They now had the authority of their own Army and Navy to support any body of law that they would choose to establish. They proceeded to invalidate the Declaration of Independence and their previous twelve years of labor and sacrifice.

Although we attach a great deal of significance to our Declaration of Independence, we must understand that this Declaration and all declarations are irrelevant to any other groups exercising political authority. They only serve as red flags waved in the face of institutional authority. Everyone that declared their independence from England in 1776 was promoting and partaking in an insurrection against established and lawful authority. This type of action can only result in civil war. Both sides call themselves patriots. But the established society calls the revolutionists rebels, while the revolutionists call the ruling government despots and demagogues.

Our history has two examples of insurrection and civil war. The rebels of 1776 succeeded in declaring their independence by raising an army sufficient to establish the authority that arises from superior arms. Superior arms, however, defeated the Confederate States of America in 1865, and therefore their declaration of independence has failed to establish a date from which to record the birth of a new nation.

Declarations of independence and constitutions are words on paper; they carry absolutely no authority. From their very beginning and throughout their existence their authority arises either from voluntary assent of the citizenry, or force of arms to compel dissenters to act in accordance with existing law. A nation is made whole everyday, by assent or by force.

The following are excerpts from the U.S. Constitution, which will demonstrate the conflict between the Declaration and the Constitution.

Article 1, Section 8:
The Congress shall have power...} {...To provide for calling forth the Militia to execute the Laws of the Union, suppress Insurrections and repel Invasions;

Article 1, Section 9:
The Privilege of the Writ of Habeas Corpus shall not be suspended, unless when in Cases of Rebellion or Invasion the public Safety may require it.

Article 3, Section 1:
No State shall enter into any Treaty, Alliance, or Confederation; grant Letters of Marque and Reprisal; coin Money; emit Bills of Credit; make any Thing but gold and silver Coin a Tender in Payment of debts; pass any Bill of Attainder, ex post facto Law, or Law impairing the Obligation of Contracts, or grant any Title of Nobility

No State shall, without the consent of the Congress, lay any Imposts or Duties on Imports or Exports, except what may be absolutely necessary for executing its inspection laws: and the net Produce of all Duties and Imposts, laid by any State on Imports or Exports, shall be for the use of the Treasury of the United States; and all such Laws shall be subject to the Revision and control of the Congress.

No State shall, without the Consent of Congress, lay any Duty of Tonnage, keep Troops, or Ships of War in time of Peace, enter into any Agreement or Compact with another State, or with a foreign Power, or engage in War, unless actually invaded, or in such imminent Danger as will not admit of delay.

Article 3, Section 3:

Treason against the United States, shall consist only in levying War against them, or in adhering to their Enemies, giving them Aid and Comfort. No person shall be convicted of Treason unless on the Testimony of two witnesses to the same overt act, or on Confession in open Court.

Article 4, Section 3:

New States may be admitted by the congress into this Union; but no new state shall be formed or erected within the Jurisdiction of any other state; nor any state be formed by junction of two or more States or Parts of States, without the Consent of the Legislatures of the States concerned as well as the Congress.

The Congress shall have power to dispose of and make all needful Rules and Regulations respecting the Territory or their Property belonging to the United States and nothing in this Constitution shall be construed as to Prejudice any Claims of the United States or of any particular State.

Article 4, Section 4:

The United States shall guarantee to every State in this Union a Republican Form of

Government, and shall protect each of them
against Invasion; and on Application of the
Legislature, or of the Executive (when the
Legislature cannot be convened) against domestic
Violence.

Article 5:
        The Congress, whenever two thirds of both
houses shall deem it necessary, shall propose
Amendments to this Constitution, or, on the
Application of the Legislatures or two thirds of the
several States, shall call a Convention for
proposing Amendments, which in either Case,
shall be valid to all Intents and Purposes, as Part
of this Constitution, when ratified by the
Legislatures of three fourths of the several
States, or be Conventions in three fourths
thereof, as the one or the other Mode of
Ratification may be proposed by the Congress.

        These are the several areas of Constitutional law
that are in direct conflict with the guarantees of the
Declaration. In Article 1, Section 8, the national
government is given the right to establish and call forth
the militia (armed forces) ". . . to execute the laws of
the union, suppress insurrections . . ." Such laws are
extremely contrary to all peoples declared right to
abolish the government over themselves, and their
declared right to establish new laws of their own
choosing. The United States was born out of the moral
illegality of the British using military forces to enforce
unpopular laws. How quickly the founding fathers forgot
that governments do not have the right to militarily
oppress any citizens of any country, including their own.
Nor have any governments the right to militarily
suppress any people's efforts to separate themselves
from old government, and establish new government for
their own benefit and happiness; might does not make
right.
        In Article 1, Section 9, we see that the
Constitution gives the authority to the government to
suspend the Writ of Habeas Corpus and to imprison
persons whom the government considers to be in
rebellion. But rebellion is a declared right, guaranteed

by the Declaration and "Nature's God," which people may invoke in order to pursue the unalienable rights of life, liberty, and the pursuit of happiness. To pass a law against rebellion, is to admit that unpopular governments have a right to suppress those they govern; or that a government representing a majority has the right to oppress and suppress minorities, enslaving them to the will of others. Popular governments, serving all the people, have no need to fear rebellion, and therefore no need of any laws against it. Rebellion was the indispensable midwife in this nation's birth. The conflict between the Declaration of Independence and the Constitution cannot be greater than that associated with the right of rebellion. The people will fashion the mode of government by which they will assent to act toward each other.

In Article 1, Section 10, the Constitution expressly forbids the various states from exercising the rights that the Declaration declared they should retain, that all peoples have the right to unite in the manner they choose and to exercise all the rights of an independent nation.

In Article 3, Section 3, the Constitution gives the government the right to accuse its citizens of the act of treason, if they commit acts of friendship towards nations defined by Congress to be enemies. The Declaration of Independence guarantees that any group of people have the right to be independent and self-determining, and to " . . .have full power to levy war, conclude peace, contract alliances . . ." In other words the Declaration makes treason an impossible act to commit when establishing a new society.

In Article 4, Section 3, The Constitution gives the government the right to admit new states to the Union, but prohibits any state from dividing, on its own, into more states. It also gives the government the right to colonize and claim jurisdiction to lands outside of its first boundary. This is not only contrary to the expressed themes of the Declaration; it is also contrary to the spirit of the Declaration. This section of the Constitution gives the United States the right to colonize wilderness territory, a right that the American Colonies rebelled against when England claimed it.

In Article 4, Section 4, all states are guaranteed a

194

republican form of government and protection against foreign and domestic violence. Again, this is contrary to the Declaration's guarantee of the right to self-determination for all people. Included in the right of self-determination is the right of minorities to resort to violence when the republican form of government is oppressive or unresponsive to the needs of those minorities. The Revolutionary War was fought because of the ideas expressed in the Declaration of Independence, opening the door for that kind of action forever more.

In Article 5, the Constitution allows for amendments to be added to the Constitution, providing three-fourths of the states ratify them. Even this article is contrary to the spirit of the Declaration, because it allows majorities to oppress minorities. The colonists exclaimed loudly against taxation without representation. If representatives had been sent to the English Parliament on behalf of the colonists, the majority in Parliament would have overruled their petitions and levied the taxes anyway. Most colonists were looked on as second-class British subjects, just as the colonists looked on Blacks and Indians as second-class citizens. The right of majorities to oppress by amendment or to refuse to liberate by amendment, may be republican, but is certainly immoral. It is contrary to the Declaration's guaranteed right to separation and independence for minorities, especially when petitions for redress go unanswered.

One must understand that the Constitution did not follow from the Declaration of Independence, but rather the Constitution followed from the Articles of Confederation. The Confederation formed out of the necessity of war that the Colonies form a government to raise an army and navy capable of fighting the British. This does not elevate the Constitution to a position of authority over activities that preceded and promoted its formation. Thomas Paine, in his book Rights of Man, tells us that constitutions are formed and agreed too, so that governments can be formed to enact laws to control commerce and social activities. Governments do not precede constitutions in a democratic environment. And constitutions do not precede the independence of people who wish to govern themselves. In all cases, any people forming a government must declare their independence from any other government, giving precedence of power for the creation of government to that Declaration. A declaration of independence is the freedom to act within the fundamental principal of government, "Do unto others as you would have them do unto you"; to establish the wisdom we wish to embody in a constitution; and to form a government to apply that wisdom to control our socio-economic interactions.

The fundamental purpose of a declaration of independence is to promote the establishment of government. It does not exclude any type of government. The Constitution, on the other hand, does forbid all activities associated with the idea of establishing government, separate from and equal to the United States Government. The United States Government would make war on anyone participating in the establishing of independent government, as history has shown. We can only conclude that the mutual exclusivity of these Documents lies fully with the Constitution. There is no justification whatsoever for this oppressive language in the Constitution. Government should respond to the will of the people. If there is conflict of will, then there must be arbitration and compromise, or there must be separation and the establishment of independent government.

Every society, every organization, every congregation, has a constitution that expresses and explains the rules and bylaws that establish the manner in which each group is to govern itself. Various and sundry constitutions are both desirable and necessary to fulfill the needs of human societies. The flaw in our National Constitution is that those who are elected to the public trust, by a majority, are given the power to attack, incarcerate, and punish people over whom they have absolutely no authority, morally or by precedent. In fact, the Declaration of Independence is precedent that no such authority can exist, but to the pain and suffering of Creation.

The inclusion into the Constitution of language that allows authoritarian interference by majorities into the political and social actions of minorities is turning out to be one of the undoings of American society.

196

Majorities have for 200 years used that authority (many times very oppressively) to keep minorities from seceding, from forming labor unions, from voting, etc.

Because we live in communities, and because our communities are often founded on moral and ethical principles of behavior, stemming from various religious heritages, we must accept, even pursue political autonomy for the community, keeping our great social alliance for economic and security purposes only.

The Constitution is not a perfect instrument of government; while continual changes in our social philosophies render it less perfect; but it was mistakenly crafted to be very difficult to change. Who, that are alive today, have elected a representative to a Constitutional Convention? Whose representative has voted to uphold each part of the Constitution, or has voted to replace parts with new articles that have more correspondence with today's social problems and obligations? Your representative took an oath to uphold a manner of maintaining government and is thus limited to forming laws that cannot be in conflict with the Constitution. Any law that is deemed by the courts to be in conflict is void and un-enforceable.

England is said to not have a constitution, because every law passed by Parliament displaces or voids older laws that are in conflict with the new law. In England the will of the people today, as expressed through their representatives today, is the law, and cannot be superseded by the past. In the United States, the Constitution cannot be changed unless 75% of the various state legislatures agree to the proposed changes. A new law, not in conflict with the Constitution, only needs a simple majority to become law. A new law desired by the people but in conflict with a Constitution embodied and empowered by men long since dead, must be set aside, until and unless that Constitution is amended to remove any conflicts with such a law. The dead have power that the living should envy.

Americans are fond of their democratic heritage, often referring to majority rule as the foundation of our social laws. But 74% of the living, desiring a change in the way society will form laws and hold itself accountable, are not enough to overcome the desires of 26% who would benefit more by leaving the Constitution

197

as structured by the dead. This is not majority rule, unless one considers the dead more wise than the living, and better able to formulate the manner of making laws, as well as the breadth and depth of laws.

Those who say that we must make it very hard to amend the Constitution are suggesting that we do not have government by the people, and for the people. They suggest that factions run our government and that some prosper more, at the expense of others. They would have us believe that operating on a basis like England, where every new law would automatically become part of the Constitution, would make it easier for some faction to take complete control of the country and take away the rights of others. However, in such an instance the majority could quickly regain their sovereignty and just powers by changing the law. America is controlled politically and economically by a faction that uses the near impossibility of changing the Constitution as a political shield for their economic power. The difficulty in changing the Constitution is a curse, not a blessing. And if social oppression continues, the Constitution will be replaced via many declarations of independence.

We must be allowed to have governments that promote and protect our moral philosophies. Treaties such as the Constitution serve to establish commerce and communication externally, where different political structures interface. But internally our Constitution is allowing the guise of individual opportunity to control commerce for the benefit of business, and morality to be diluted.

If the Constitution is alive, then it must function for all of the people. If it cannot function for all of the people, then it must be altered to do so or be replaced with new constitutions for the benefit and protection of the communities who have it in their interest to be self-determining. Self-determination has gone too far in defining individual rights, and not nearly far enough in defining community rights.

The Constitution's originators assumed that the individual would always support the community he or she belonged to, or move to one that they could support. So the language of the Constitution is made to favor the individual. But in today's world, individuals out

198

of sync with their community do not move to more harmonious situations. Instead they enlist the aid of the courts and the language of the Constitution to pursue not only an individual, but also a non-communal philosophy. They force acceptance of their behavior onto a community that does not desire their presence. To be truly individual is to be singularly self-determining, to be a nation unto oneself. This is only a worthy goal of anarchists, and should not be a political or judicial goal of our government.

The prisons that hold those deemed to have transgressed some social law are not the place to measure society's ability to establish and maintain harmony. More and more prisons demonstrate a failed social government. These prisons are microcosms of the great prison that society is to itself. While the majority of citizens have become economic prisoners of the political elite, who today does not feel imprisoned by the threat of violence against their person and property, at home and in public? The number of prisoners incarcerated is a signpost of the economic despair and social corruption increasing in our society. We segregate them in the hope of purifying that which decays, because it is imperfect by design, and kept imperfect by a political-industrial conspiracy of greed and profit in place of social fairness.

Below are some excerpts from Tom Paine's book "Rights of Man." They are forever timely.

"Reason and Ignorance, the opposite to each other, influence the great bulk of mankind. If either of these can be rendered sufficiently extensive in a country, the machinery of Government goes easily on. Reason obeys itself; and Ignorance submits to whatever is dictated to it."

"Whether the forms and maxims of Governments which are still in practice were adapted to the condition of the world at the period they were established is not in this case the question. The older they are the less correspondence can they have with the present state of things.

Time, and change of circumstances and opinions,

have the same progressive effect in rendering modes of Government obsolete as they have upon customs and manners. Agriculture, commerce, manufactures, and the tranquil arts, by which the prosperity of Nations is best promoted, require a different system of Government, and a different species of knowledge to direct its operations, than what might have been required in the former condition of the world.

From what we now see, nothing of reform in the political world ought to be held improbable. It is an age of Revolutions, in which everything may be looked for."

"It is for the good of Nations and not for the emolument or aggrandizement of particular individuals, that Government ought to be established, and that mankind are at the expense of supporting it. The defects of every Government and Constitution, both as to principle and form, must on a parity of reasoning, be as open to discussion as the defects of a law, and it is a duty which every man owes to society to point them out. When those defects, and the means of remedying them, are generally seen by a Nation, that Nation will reform its Government or its Constitution in the one case, as the Government repealed or reformed the law in the other. The operation of Government is restricted to the making and the administering of laws; but it is to a Nation (the citizens) that the right of forming or reforming, generating or regenerating, Constitutions and Governments belong; and consequently those subjects, as subjects of investigations, are always before a country as a matter of right, and cannot, without invading the general rights of that country, be made subjects for prosecution."

Chapter 18 - Opinion

I protest! I protest your actions, your wealth, your laziness, your war mongering, your different religions, your drug culture, your social corruption, your selfishness, your John Birch redneckedness, and your libertine anarchy. There really are few things about your philosophy and behavior that I do not protest.

Wait a minute. Don't get so upset. I really don't protest your being that much. In fact, I really do not understand protesting. I do have opinions, and I even value them as a source of self-esteem. But then I presume that you do likewise. Though I may not value your opinion, I accept that mine likewise is a fairly worthless commodity.

How is it we have so many people in the streets cajoling or berating us with their various opinions? Do these people believe that their opinions should be held in higher esteem by the rest of society, who may have different opinions? These people are implying that my beliefs are wrong. That all my years of gathering data, by which I formulate my various opinions is deficient. I admit it may be a different data-set by which I formulate my beliefs, but it is not anymore deficient than theirs. If that is not a fact, it is at least my opinion.

We can all say with equal validity, "See as I see, believe as I believe, or you are in error." To protest the actions or beliefs of others, because we believe them to be in error, is to accept with equal weight the protest of our own actions and beliefs by others, because they believe we are in error. We cannot escape this circle of interaction. To avoid social friction and the negative social results of public protests, we should act in a manner such that if we believe differently, we should, with great resolve, live differently. We should congregate with those who believe similar to ourselves, and establish a separate society to demonstrate our different philosophy. The success of our separate society will be sufficient protest of the philosophies of those who believe differently. The failure of our separate society would be a sufficient lesson and protest of our deficient philosophy. In either case we would not be engaging in an un-winnable public argument over our opinions.

Many public protests appear to be more like religious evangelism, but aimed at supporting some form of government rather than the Creator. They do so in an effort to lobby for political support, which is often for sale for future votes or campaign funds. However, public protests do not render them to be better than the argument of those who oppose them. And they often lead to social conflict. At least in forming separate societies we may establish treaties of behavior between our separate societies that recognize that differences in social beliefs are not only permissible, but sacrosanct. The fundamental principle of government, "Do unto others as you would have them do unto you", does not provide a foundation from which we may believe we have a superior philosophy that others should be made aware of, without our accepting the validity of that same premise when it is held by those we believe to be in error. We either live by the fundamental principle of government, or we believe ourselves to have Satan's blessing, also known as Divine authority, to force our opinions upon others; denying the equal validity of all philosophies to exercise the right of autonomy. The world has had hundreds of years of missionaries violating this fundamental principle of government. One must presume that their ignorance of fundamental principles and their desire to pursue a path of protest and destruction of dissimilar philosophies is evidence of their falsehood, and the reason our societies along with their religions are decaying; and that they are powerless to thwart that decay. Perhaps the Creator walks a different path, or has created many paths of approach into light, without the need to exclude other philosophies, or to abandon fundamental principles.

This is not to say that we are all righteous, serving truth, and living reality in the expression of our philosophies. Many of our philosophies are in error and will have to be altered or abolished, when we obtain or are willing to receive more information from experience of what works and what does not work. Many of the current difficulties that seem to occur between groups of dissimilar philosophies, have more to do with differences of opinion on how we should relate to the Earth and its resources, and how we should relate to other life-forms and their requirements. The difference in moral philosophies between ourselves, which seem to have always been precarious in the area of how we should relate to each other, is now being strained by the expansion and pressure of these new issues. It is not likely that we can maintain a status quo, which has never existed to begin with. In fact, we appear to be accelerating beyond our capacity to develop any consensus that would allow us to develop cohesive social relationships.

This brings to mind the story of a group of people wishing to move across an unknown wilderness in search of a new home. They chose a leader and then set out upon their journey. They soon discovered that some younger members were impatient and surged ahead of the main group. Another group of older persons was uncertain of their future and did not want so quick a change; they lagged behind. The leader was forced to divide his time between three groups, trying to give them all the guidance and direction they required. As their journey continued, these groups moved further apart until they lost sight of each other. The leader was unable to assist any of them, so anarchy broke out in each group and they all perished in the wilderness.

Politically, our society is becoming much like this group of people. We are failing to be, or become, one people. Our leadership is unable to respond adequately to our needs, to insure that we can survive our journey through life's trials and tribulations. If we cannot agree to be one society with one set of leaders, then we must be separate societies with separate leadership. Much of what divides our society is based on beliefs and opinions from our youth and prevents us from understanding the beliefs of others. So our social interactions often lead to argument and protests that neither end, nor resolve our differences

Imagine that two people are discussing philosophy and an issue of social concern is brought up, upon which the two people soon discover they have vastly different opinions. The first person has the perception that all of us are at the edge of a cliff; that we are balancing on stilts; the wind is blowing hard at our backs and we may be blown over the cliff at any moment. The first person not only perceives this condition as reality, he believes that the second person need only open his eyes to behold that same reality. He cannot understand why the second person cannot appreciate their predicament and join him in recognizing an obvious solution to these difficulties. The second person feels that we are all standing on solid ground, with no cliffs nearby, and only a gentle breeze is blowing. This second person not only perceives his opinion as reality; it is beyond his ability to understand what the first person is so upset about.

The principle that follows from this analogy is that perceptions are not only very often different, but are also very difficult to convey. A great deal of our perceptions and judgments come from what we were taught at home, school, and church. We develop biases based on our particular cultural heritage and we are compelled, by all that we are, to defend our biases publicly and privately. Where we fail in our public relationships is in not understanding that how we perceive reality, may be very different from how others perceive reality. We all hold that there is only one reality and we are privy to its content. These differences may be beyond any immediate verbal translation, causing the parties at dispute to remain in dispute. Quite often anger and frustration on both sides act as a second compelling force to keep the sides apart.

The inability of different peoples to perceive the universe in the same way will always be a challenge for the future. We must work out to our own satisfaction the things that serve us well, and abandon the things that prove in time to be in conflict with our goals and peaceful relationships with other cultures. We must socially support fact over opinion whenever possible.